Vanishing Treasures

National Park Service
U.S. Department of the Interior

Vanishing Treasures Program

Partnership Issue

I0430086

Year-End Report
Fiscal Year 2008 and
Funded Projects for 2009

Acknowledgments:

Executive Editor: Virginia Salazar-Halfmoon

Editor-in Chief: Randy Skeirik

Contributing Editors: Jake Barrow

Advisor: Sande McDermott

All reports and photographs were provided by park
VT staff unless otherwise credited.

State maps were produced by the NPS Intermountain
Region Geographic Resources Program, Denver, CO.

Cover Photo: The corral and cattle chute at Gachado Line Camp near the Mexican border in Organ Pipe Cactus National Monument Photo: Randall Skeirik

Table of Contents

Message from the Vanishing Treasures Program Manager

A major focus of the Vanishing Treasures Leadership Committee(VT LC) this year was the revision of the VT Charter. After careful consideration, pen was put to paper and the revised Charter was accepted and signed by the Regional Directors (RDs) of both the Intermountain and Pacific West Regions. Leadership Chair Corky Hays, along with the appropriate regional VT representative, accompanied me to present the revised Charter to the Regional Directors. Both RDs continue to strongly support the VT Program and expressed their belief that significant resource preservation has resulted from the program's efforts and focus. They also recoginze that what makes the Program unique, and strengthens it role in the NPS, are the cultural connections that are fostered between the resources themselves and associated local and traditional communities. Both Directors emphasized the need to continue our focus on the philosophy of preservation, and to expand our capabilities through partnering.

In early September 2008, the Vanishing Treasures Program received national exposure when the Associated Press article "Ruins in Ruin" was printed and received national distribution. This article resulted in great public interest in VT, and we received numerous offers of financial and partnering support for the Program.

Encouraged by this response, we have been exploring the possibility of creating a "friends" group for Vanishing Treasures. With this in mind, I attended the Association of Partners for Public Lands (APPL) Conference. It was eye-opening to see the amount of work that is being accomplished on federal lands through partnerships and partnering efforts. At the same time, I learned that establishing a friends organization for a multi-park program such as VT would be unique since, typically, friends groups are designed to support individual parks. The unique characteristics of such a partnership have required ongoing legal fact-finding as we work to develop a partnership mechanism that can support VT Program efforts. Despite these challenges, a program-wide friends group, or some other form of partnership venue, continues to be a high priority for the Program.

In addition to my attendance at the APPL conference, the superintendent of the San Antonio Missions National Historical Park (SAAN) presented a session to the VT LC on SAAN's successful partnership efforts when we met in San Antonio. The primary message he delivered was that while friends organizations and partnerships can initially be very time consuming, once the right people are in place, amazing work can be accomplished when working toward common goals.

In May, the Vanishing Treasures Program cosponsored the IMR Comprehensive Resource Stewardship Conference. The goal of this conference was to foster a holistic view of resource management issues and not artificially separate cultural and natural resource impacts. The VT Program coordinated with the Archeology Program for a day of pre-conference Affinity Meetings that were well attended. Many interesting topics were presented, some of which included natural resource components. It was a great opportunity for VT staff from many disparate parks to meet and exchange information.

A continuing objective of the VT Program is to pro-actively offer assistance to the parks in the program that may not have received substantial support from VT in the past. This support may take the form of help in developing and implementing PMIS projects or through Technical Assistance site visits. This year, Gila Cliff Dwellings National Monument (GICL) received a team visit from the VT Program staff. The primary purpose of the visit was to provide a condition assessment of the main cliff dwellings and outlying sites that were identified by the Superintendent. We were able to research and identify restored portions of the sites to assist the park with preservation planning efforts, and we found that all of the sites within the park are in very stable condition. The superintendent also coordinated an assessment of a heavily visited site in the adjacent USFS Gila Wilderness. Unfortunately we found that the USFS site had suffered significant damage. The Vanishing Treasures team prepared a report for the USFS archeologists outlining various preservation strategies.

With the support of the leadership, the VT Program intends to continue to offer on-site assessment support to parks that may not have benefitted from VT funding in the past. In addition, under the leadership of Jake Barrow, we are currently finalizing the Preservation and Management Guidelines for Vanishing Treasures Resources. Look for this new resource to be completed and distributed within the year.

Virginia Salazar-Halfmoon
Virginia Salazar-Halfmoon
Vanishing Treasures Program Manager

At-Large VT Program Staff

Preston Fisher, Structural Engineer

Although I am stationed at Mesa Verde, 80% of my time is intended to be spent serving the needs of the other 44 parks in the VT Program.

At Mesa Verde, I served as the Contracting Officer's Representative (COR) on a contract to replace site shelter panels at Sun Point Surface Site shelter on the Mesa Top Loop at Mesa Verde.

I provided assistance to a number of VT parks, including:

- Aztec Ruins National Monument - Evaluated recent cracking observed at the Great Kiva. Recommended a monitoring strategy and assisted with installation and monitoring of the monitor points;
- Lake Meredith National Recreation Area – Evaluated conditions at McBride Ranch House and made preservation and stabilization recommendations;
- Casa Grande Ruins National Monument – Downloaded data from crack meters and data loggers installed in 2007. Evaluated the data and determined there has been no significant movement at any of the monitoring points to date;
- Tonto National Monument – Evaluated potential moisture problems that may be associated with a fault running through the Lower Dwelling. Provided recommendations for monitoring the upper retaining wall at the Lower Dwelling during subsurface investigations behind the wall;
- Montezuma Castle National Monument – Evaluated structural condition of some cracked vigas throughout the site and recommended placement of supports in areas where foot traffic on upper levels are damaging roofs in rooms below;

- Zion National Park – Evaluated structural stability of Cable Mountain draw works and made preservation and stabilization recommendations;
- Canyonlands National Park – Evaluated and made stabilization recommendations for several sites along the Green River Corridor;
- Chaco Culture National Historical Park – Inspected conditions and evaluated the effectiveness of structural supports installed in the 1970's.
- Carlsbad Caverns National Park – Evaluated structural condition of CCC era historical buildings and made stabilization and rehabilitation recommendations.
- Gila Cliff Dwellings National Monument – Participated in VT Team assessment of the Gila Cliff Dwellings and, in cooperation with US Forest Service (USFS) staff, contributed to an assessment of the Cosgrove Site on USFS land near the Gila Cliff Dwellings.

In addition, I partnered with the Bureau of Land Management (BLM) to review stabilization and preservation methods and activities for the Fairbanks Mercantile Building near Tombstone, AZ, making recommendations for structural stability issues in its south bay; I participated in a Job Fair at Fort Lewis College in Durango, CO; and attended VT backfilling discussions that were held at Aztec Ruins NM in April, 2008. I also attended the VT Leadership Committee meeting in San Antonio, TX, and organized and moderated two discussion panels for the Intermountain Region (IMR) Comprehensive Resource Stewardship Conference that was held in Tucson, AZ in May.

I am excited to be a part of the VT Program as it transitions into the 21st century. I continue to be available to VT parks to provide assistance in evaluating and monitoring the structural integrity of their resources, and developing and recommending actions that can be taken to stabilize, preserve, and protect these fragile resources.

Jake Barrow, Exhibit Specialist

FY 2008 was an active year with hardly a moment to reflect. This short piece offers an opportunity to take a larger view of the year after some months have passed. My time in the office was focused on preparing a history of ruins treatment for the *Preservation and Management Guidelines for Vanishing Treasures Resources*. While this work has been rewarding in many ways, it doesn't compete with the field activities generated from the technical assistance requests. It was a banner year.

Serving either as agreements technical representative or as consultant to the CESU process (University partnerships) had me involved at Death Valley, Fort Davis, and El Morro. The Death Valley projects, being accomplished by the University of Vermont (UVM) Heritage Program in Engineering, are focused on two very important challenges, both addressing issues of wood deterioration and preservation.

The first, at Keane Wonder Mine, will sort out complex engineering issues of the deteriorating timber tramway and result in a field school of applied stabilization. The second, at Scotty's Castle, is conducting primary research to find wood preservatives that will deal both with UV deterioration and water repellency while respecting the patina of age.

At Fort Davis, a summer field school (also with UVM) occurred for the fourth year in a row to preserve the Post Hospital. A two day adobe and plaster workshop open to the public was held. Overwhelming public interest resulted in an overflow crowd.

The hospital project (supported by a Save America's Treasures grant) is nearly concluded with just a few punch-out items remaining. This project preserves the original fabric and augments interpretation of that fabric with the re-introduction of floors and stabilizing compensating plasters which draw attention to original 19th fabric. While it pushes the definition of ruins stabilization, the hospital project fits, since the primary focus has been preserving the original highly authentic resources. Fort Davis has some of the richest examples of authenticity to be found in a frontier fort.

A personal highlight of the year was stabilization work at Fort Bottom Cabin in Canyonlands. Noreen Fritz organized a project focused on needed log preservation at this cabin in the back country. After planning, a team put together by the park convened at the cabin for a workshop in sill replacement, dutchman splicing, corner stabilization, pinning of posts and lintels, and Boracare treatment. Access to the site was by boat and we all camped out on the beach of the Green River. Since there was no going down to Home Depot to pick up a missing tool or supply, we all made do with what we had. It worked. What really impressed me was the "can do" attitude on the part of all there. We had some assistance from the trail crew which proved absolutely invaluable. Nothing deters that trail crew.

The University of Pennsylvania (UPenn) started a summer field school at El Morro, in which I briefly participated. This represents the 18th year of field work by the Architectural Conservation Laboratory at UPenn in the Southwest and it is always a learning experience to be associated with them. UPenn has for many years now focused on the conservation of earthen surfaces at sites within Mesa Verde. This challenging work is sure to provide beneficial results.

Other requests took me to Organ Pipe, San Antonio, Bandelier, Salinas Pueblo Missions, Aztec, Gila, Casa Grande, Pecos, Big Bend, Fort Craig for BLM, and Columbus, NM for the Landmarks Program. In addition, I managed the out-placement of the Santa Fe Conservation Lab to the State of New Mexico in a partnering venture and also oversaw a regional Volunteers in Parks program.

Randy Skeirik, Historical Architect

As has been the case over the past four years, last year was a busy one. I continued my duties as the Resource Management Division Chief at Montezuma Castle and Tuzigoot National Monuments (MOCA/TUZI) until just before the end of the fiscal year. In September a park base increase allowed us to hire a new, permanent, full-time natural resource manager who assumed the Resource Division Chief duties, relieving me of that responsibility. As a result, the end of the fiscal year found me moving into a new office, and looking forward to a drastically altered workload. For the first time since coming to the NPS, I should be able to allocate my time more along the 80/20 percent split that was envisioned when the historical architect position was first created.

Prior to all that, I began the year with a trip to the Intermountain Regional Office to sit on the concessions panel for Zion National Park. On the way, I was able to participate in an adobe workshop at the Church of San José de Gracia in Las Trampas, New Mexico that was co-sponsored by the NPS and Cornerstones Community Partnerships. In November I attended the quarterly meeting of cultural resource managers of southern Arizona parks.

The spring of 2008 began with a site visit to Organ Pipe Cactus National Monument which was followed in close succession by a week of supervisory training, technical assistance visits to Zion and Guadalupe Mountains National Parks, the VT Leadership Committee meeting in San Antonio, and a meeting of the southern Arizona National Parks with representatives of the Arizona State Historic Preservation Office (AZSHPO).

At Organ Pipe, I discussed broad preservation issues with VT archeologist Joe Tuomey, and visited several sites to make preservation recommendations. At Zion, I revisited two log cabins in Kolob Canyon, and I accompanied Supervisory Archeologist Sarah Horton to the upper terminus of the cable draw works. The draw works, a small heavy-timber structure that was used to lower lumber from the mesa down to Zion Canyon, has suffered from exposure to the elements and many of its timbers have severely deteriorated. A plan is being devised to stabilize and preserve the structure.

At Guadalupe, I had the opportunity to visit several sites including a stage stop on the Butterfield Trail, a remote ranch house, an early dugout, and a rancher's line camp. Each of these sites presented different preservation challenges and appropriate treatment recommendations were prepared for each one.

In May I attended the Intermountain Region's Comprehensive Resource Stewardship Conference that was held in Tucson. This was a great opportunity to meet and interact with natural and cultural resource staff not only from VT parks, but many parks throughout the region.

The following month I was in Phoenix to represent the VT program in a meeting of the AZSHPO and the southern Arizona Parks. Annual meetings between the SHPO and the parks are required, but had not been occurring regularly. This meeting was intended to restart that process. In July I was back in Phoenix to attend one of the regular meetings of the cultural resource managers from southern Arizona parks. As always, these meetings are informative and give all the participating parks the opportunity to meet, share information, and stay informed on the past and upcoming resource activities at the parks.

Although my desktop publishing skills continue to improve, I still find myself spending a considerable amount of time producing this report. Everyone in VT parks needs to remember to take pictures of your staff as they are performing preservation related duties so that we can show our readers what we, as a program, are accomplishing.

As always, Preston, Jake and I are all available, at no cost your park, to provide specialized technical assistance for Vanishing Treasures Resources. I am available to all VT parks to provide architectural preservation services. I can assist with the identification, research, planning, treatment, and preservation maintenance of historic and prehistoric structures. I can also help to document existing conditions, define treatment actions, and prepare historic structure reports, and I can assist parks that lack staff experienced in the preparation of VT SEPAS proposals to develop competitive project proposals.

I continue to look forward to expanding my role in both the overall management of the program and the preservation of individual VT resources.

Feature Articles

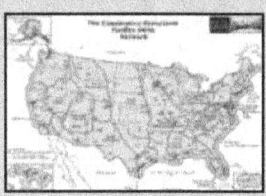

The National Park Service and Partnering: A History of Public Involvement

With the creation of the National Park Service in 1916, NPS leaders and superintendents found themselves with a handful of parks and a clearly defined mission, but only limited resources with which to get their parks under management and provide memorable visitor experiences. NPS Director Stephen Mather knew that building public support for the fledgling National Parks was crucial for their future. A creative mix of resourcefulness, philanthropy, and partnering with outside groups all contributed to the growth of the National Park system.

While resourcefulness and philanthropy still play large roles, over the last quarter century, partnerships have become increasingly important as a way to get things done, both within and beyond park boundaries. In fact, many of the parks that have been established in the last twenty-five years have clear mandates to partner, and some national parks and NPS programs operate almost exclusively through partnerships. Heritage areas and corridors, and national trails and rivers are all examples of partnership units.

The idea behind heritage areas, heritage corridors, and national trails and rivers is to offer an innovative method for citizens, working in partnership with local, state, and Federal governments, and nonprofit and private sector interests, to shape the long-term future of their communities. The partnership approach creates the opportunity for a diverse range of constituents to come together to voice a range of visions and perspectives. By definition, partners must work collaboratively to shape plans and implement strategies that will work to the benefit of all involved.

Inclusive by their very nature, partnerships foster involvement, involvement leads to awareness, and awareness leads to action, all of which encourages a culture of stewardship.

To take full advantage of the benefits of partnering, partnership management has become a core competency essential to both the NPS mission and the delivery of a higher level of public service. The challenge now facing the Park Service is to more effectively develop that competency by building on past partnership successes and developing new capacities servicewide. Our challenge, at every level, is to effectively align and leverage resources to enable NPS employees and our partners to create and sustain effective partnerships.

Throughout the National Park Service, we can find a wide range of program activities and functions that incorporate successful partnerships. Anecdotally, and in the findings of a 2001 NPS survey for the Office of Management and Budget, we know that certain parks have been especially successful in building and maintaining a strong and highly productive partnership culture. But there remains much room to improve partnering capacity throughout the NPS.

The 2001 survey also showed that parks can readily identify additional partnerships that they need to initiate or foster, as well as the under-performing partnerships that need more attention and support by trained staff. To assist parks in creating or improving partnerships the Intermountain Region (IMR) has recently hired a new full-time Partnership Coordinator, Krista Muddle.

Krista came to NPS from the Association of Partners for Public Lands (APPL) where she spent five years as the educational ser-

vices coordinator. She started her NPS service by focusing on two Intermountain Regional Partnership Roundtables. These brainstorming sessions were sponsored by the Rocky Mountain Nature Association and the Western National Parks Association, both long-standing partners. Collectively the sessions drew Executive Directors from twenty nonprofit partners and twenty IMR park superintendents.

Her coordination duties include liaising with park partners, the Washington-based Partnership office, and Interpretation offices to explore ways to expand fund raising efforts, retail operations, and other in-kind services that support our parks. At the same time, Krista also serves the cooperating associations in the Intermountain Region.

Taking a different approach, partnerships in the Pacific West Region (PWR) are managed by the Partnerships Advisory Committee. The mission of this committee is:

- to serve as a forum to build capacity for effective and sustainable partnerships to advance the missions of the parks and programs of the Pacific West Region of the National Park Service;
- to enable the PWR to demonstrate regional and national leadership in addressing trends, opportunities, issues, problems, and barriers related to effective partnering in a timely manner;
- to develop informed responses, solutions to problems, workable processes to problems and model initiatives; and
- to maintain PWR leadership in innovative, cutting edge partnering

Many parks in the Intermountain Region already work with the Western National Parks Association, but there are 17 other strong cooperating associations that are available to provide direct cash aid, interpretive products and services, and in-kind donations to these parks.

Another form of partnering, one that is available to all parks regardless of size or location, is the National Network of Cooperative Ecosystem Study Units. Cooperative Ecosystem Study Units (CESUs) were established to provide research, technical assistance, and education to federal land management, environmental, and research agencies and their potential partners.

Multiple federal agencies and universities are among the partners participating in this program. CESUs incorporate biological, physical, social, and cultural sciences that can be used to address resource issues (both natural and cultural) and provide interdisciplinary problem solving at multiple scales in an ecosystem context. Benefits of these cooperative efforts include high-quality science, usable knowledge for resource managers, responsive technical assistance, continuing education, and cost-effective research programs for Federal land management agencies, environmental and research agencies, and the nation's universities.

A number of the Vanishing Treasures funded projects described later in this Report were designed to include partnerships. You can read about these projects in the submissions from Aztec Ruins National Monument, Bandelier National Monument, Chaco Culture National Historical Park, El Malpais National Monument, Mesa Verde National Park, Navajo National Monument, and Walnut Canyon National Monument.

For additional information on partnering in the National Park Service you can contact Krista Muddle at the Intermountain Regional office (Krista_Muddle@nps.gov, 303.969.2356) or Martha Lee in the Pacific West Region (martha_lee@nps.gov, 925.838.0249).

For information on the National Network of Cooperative Ecosystem Study Units you can visit their web site at: http://www.cesu.psu.edu/.

NPS contacts for CESUs included within the Intermountain and Pacific West Regions are:

Colorado Plateau CESU

Anne Trinkle Jones, Cultural Resources Coordinator
A_Trinkle_Jones@nps.gov, 928.523.0680

Californian CESU

James Shevock, National Park Service Research Coordinator
jshevock@nature.berkeley.edu, 510.643.0665

Pacific Northwest CESU

Chris Lauver, PNW CESU Co-leader and NPS Research Coordinator
Chris_Lauver@nps.gov 206.685.7404

Great Basin CESU

Dr.. Angela Evenden, Research Coordinator, Great Basin CESU
Angela_Evenden@nps.gov, 775.784.4583

Desert Southwest CESU

Larry L. Norris, NPS Southwest Research Coordinator
lnorris@ag.arizona.edu, 520.621.7998

Rocky Mountain CESU

Kathy Tonnessen, Natural Resources Research Coordinator
kathy.tonnessen@cfc.umt.edu, 406.243.4449

Great Plains CESU

Gary Willson, Research Coordinator
gary_willson@nps.gov, 402.472.5047

Gulf Coast CESU

Louise Hose ,Primary Contact
lhose@ag.tamu.edu, 979.845.9787

CONSERVATION AND FIELD STUDY AT THE UNIVERSITY OF VERMONT: CESU AND RESOURCE PRESERVATION IN VANISHING TREASURES PARKS

Douglas Porter, School of Engineering, University of Vermont

Since 2002, the University of Vermont has hosted a series of field study projects designed to advance the field of historic preservation through the development of pilot and model conservation treatments. Many of these projects involve federal agencies as project cooperators and are administered by the Pacific Northwest CESU Program through the University of Washington. Field study projects provide opportunities for students to complete degree requirements while becoming familiar with current conservation technologies and developing employment prospects with project partners. Initially conducted within the Graduate Program for Historic Preservation, in 2005 the field study program was expanded to include students from the School of Engineering as well. Today the program operates within the School of Engineering, though students from both programs continue to be involved.

The projects include conservation research, design, and implementation, combining traditional trades (e.g., adobe making, plastering, period millwork production, brick and stone masonry) with preservation technologies (e.g., non-destructive evaluation, materials testing, sensors and structural monitoring, and treatment design). Three of the project sites are in Vanishing Treasures parks including the Post Hospital at Fort Davis National Historic Site, and Scotty's Castle and Keane Wonder Mine, both in Death Valley National Park. The work at Fort Davis was focused on the stabilization and partial restoration of the adobe Post Hospital, a key interpretive site within the Park. At Scotty's Castle, the project includes condition assessment and both laboratory and in situ testing of conservation treatments for redwood architectural elements on the nine buildings of the Scotty's Castle complex. This year, work at Death Valley National Park was expanded to include engineering evaluation and emergency stabilization of the aerial tramway at Keane Wonder Mine. All of these projects are multi-year efforts. Work at Scotty's Castle and Keane Wonder Mine is ongoing.

At Fort Davis National Historic Site, a series of field school projects (2005-2008) focused on stabilizing surviving historic fabric, improving public access and interpretation, and partially restoring the envelope of the historic Post Hospital. The scope of work included the conservation of historic plasters; reconstruction and reinstatement of missing millwork (primarily doors, windows, and floors) critical to the preservation and interpretation of the building; and adobe repairs and application of a compensating plaster in areas where historic plaster no longer survives. Working with NPS, the university assembled a project staff specialized in the conservation technologies and traditional trades necessary to complete the work. Each field school generated student internship positions. Interns were selected from the Historic Preservation Program and the School of Engineering at the University of Vermont, as well as from similar programs at other universities. In addition to the internships, training was also made available to graduates of university programs, owners of adobe homes in nearby communities, and practicing professional conservators. A portion of the work was conducted as a Vanishing Treasures training program, so that NPS personnel participated in the training as well. Non-profit partners included Cornerstones Community Partnerships an organization dedicated to the preservation

Trainees learn to make adobes at Fort Davis NHS.
Photo: Iannis Avrimides

of architectural heritage and community traditions throughout the Greater Southwest working to revitalize communities and affirm cultural values.

Scotty's Castle, an estate built by Chicago millionaire Albert Johnson in the 1920s, is located within Death Valley National Park. While Scotty's Castle is not a Vanishing Treasures site, it is in a VT park and is likely to yield results useful at VT sites. Most of the wooden architectural features on the exteriors of the nine surviving buildings are made of redwood and date from the time of original construction. More than 80 years of exposure to the harsh desert environment has damaged the exterior woodwork. The School of Engineering at the University of Vermont is assisting the Park in the investigation of treatments that will help protect the wood from weathering due to ultraviolet exposure. To achieve this goal, the University of Vermont and Park staff participated in a conditions survey and assessment of over 3,000 exterior redwood elements on the buildings. Based on the conditions encountered in the field, the University conducted a review of current literature and developed a testing program for evaluation of UV and visible light stabilizing treatments. The testing program includes accelerated and natural weathering tests, in situ treatment testing, and pilot treatment of selected portions of the woodwork. Student research assistants have been involved in all aspects of site work, development of a survey database, literature review, and the testing program. The accelerated weathering test was recently completed, and sample coupons have been installed in a weathering rack on site. Project participants are evaluating test results, and treatment of a portion of the estate woodwork is scheduled for the 2009/10 winter season.

In 2009, the School of Engineering began work with the National Park Service and professional partners on the assessment and initial stabilization of the aerial tramway at the Keane Wonder Mine, a gold mine active between 1903 and 1916. In 2008 the NPS closed the site to public access due to safety concerns; until then it was one of the most frequently visited mine sites in the Park. The project includes a structural evaluation of the tramway towers, terminals and contiguous structures; a wood assessment to identify wood species, determine the allowable grade for comparison to the engineering requirements, and quantify remaining sound wood; and design and implementation of repairs and stabilization strategies. The University of Vermont assembled a team consisting of a wood scientist, a structural engineer, an architectural conservator, a preservation specialist, and a student research assistant to conduct condition assessment and determine repair needs of the tramway; this team may be expanded in the future in order to work on other sites within the park. Fieldwork was done with assistance from the Vanishing Treasures Engineer, Historical Architect, and staff and volunteers from the park. Repairs will be addressed through a field school that will focus on training park staff and students in the repair techniques to be implemented.

The field school program at the University of Vermont has produced measurable benefits for parks and students. The research facilities of the university have been brought to bear on specific problems occurring in the parks, treatment strategies have been developed, pilot treatments have been conducted, and in some cases repair work is underway. Scores of students have participated in grant-funded project activities on nationally significant sites through class projects, research assistantships, and internships. In addition, field study projects have served as the basis for thesis research, and cooperation with federal and non-profit partners has created employment opportunities for graduating students.

An important and unique aspect of our experience at the University of Vermont is that structural and civil engineering have taken increasingly prominent roles in these projects. Field schools were originally conducted by the Historic Preservation program. As the work became more technically demanding, it encouraged interdisciplinary collaboration between the Historic Preservation program and the School of Engineering. Engineering faculty and practicing professionals began to participate directly in some of the projects, both at research and treatment implementation

The assessment crew working on the aerial tramway, Keane Wonder Mine, April 2009.
Photo: Douglas Porter

levels, which created opportunities for students to study and use new technologies (e.g., nondestructive evaluation of structural woodwork, measurement of axial loads in iron truss elements, etc). In 2006, I moved from the Historic Preservation program to the School of Engineering and began operating the field projects as a program of the School. The School began using historic sites for student projects in Geotechnical Design and Senior Capstone courses. A colloquium on the development of heritage preservation engineering curricula is scheduled for June 2009 as the School of Engineering continues to develop heritage preservation engineering as a new area of focus.

The application of engineering techniques to historic buildings, materials, and structural systems present a number of unique challenges that are seldom addressed in university programs. Many of these challenges are the result of a commitment to preserving the authenticity and historic integrity of heritage structures on the one hand, and ensuring public safety on the other. American universities have been slow to develop curricula focused on heritage education for engineering students, and as a consequence students are not receiving training in many of the issues encountered in ruins stabilization. But as the roles that engineers play in historic preservation become more prominent, universities must take the lead in teaching and research focused on quantitative techniques and methodologies applied to the engineering evaluation and remediation of heritage structures. Participation in field study projects, like those occurring in Vanishing Treasures parks, have helped the University of Vermont to begin to address this issue.

Acknowledgments: I would like to thank our project partners at Fort Davis National Historic Site and Death Valley National Park, Vanishing Treasures staff, our non-profit partners, and the students and volunteers who have devoted so much time and energy to making these projects successful.

UNIVERSITY OF NEW MEXICO

The School of Architecture and Planning at the University of New Mexico (UNM) is exploring opportunities for field study in the western parks. Field study projects will be conducted in conjunction with UNM's Historic Preservation and Regionalism Program. Research Associate Professor Douglas Porter is taking the lead in developing these projects. Candidate projects should be focused on preservation technologies and traditional trades used in the conservation of archeological and historic sites in the west, and should create internships, research assistantships, and/or capstone projects for students enrolled in the program. For more information, please contact Douglas Porter at:

The University of New Mexico, School of Architecture and Planning
MSC04 2530
Albuquerque, NM 87131-0001
(802) 324-7528
Douglas_Porter@myfairpoint.net

Vanishing Treasures: Experiences from a University Partner

R. Brooks Jeffery, College of Architecture and Landscape Architecture, The University of Arizona

Introduction

The Preservation Studies program at the University of Arizona, College of Architecture and Landscape Architecture has maintained a relationship with the National Park Service since 2000 through the Cooperative Ecosystem Studies Unit (CESU) program. This relationship has allowed all the participants – parks, university programs, and students – to enter into a win-win-win situation by providing opportunities for training, introduction to the National Park Service as a career, and a financial mechanism to support preservation programs such as ours. Because of the geographic location of our program, many of the parks in which we work are Vanishing Treasures parks where the students can be exposed to the critical issues and unique challenges of cultural resources management in the arid West. Our program also addresses the need for training the next generation of park professionals to replace the vanishing human treasures. This paper summarizes the experiences of this nearly 10-year relationship between the National Park Service, the Vanishing Treasures program, and the University of Arizona as well as a profile of one of this relationship's signature projects, the Missions Initiative, then concludes with generalized observations based on these experiences.

Preservation Studies at the University of Arizona

Since the 1970s, the University of Arizona's Preservation Studies program has been at the forefront of preservation issues facing buildings, cities, and landscapes of the Greater Southwest, defined by the southwestern United States and northwestern Mexico. From the Pueblo and Hohokam prehistoric cultures and the Spanish Colonial missions, presidios, and towns to the American Territorial vernacular built environment and 20th century revival and modern influences, this region is saturated with cultural resources of international significance creating a fluid landscape that is constantly remaking itself.

The mission of the Preservation Studies program is to educate students in the preservation of the built environment as part of a comprehensive conservation ethic. Through curricular, research, and outreach activities, the program is:

Interdisciplinary, teaching holistic problem-solving within an integrated environment of natural and cultural resources;

Inter-institutional, promoting collaborative engagement between public and private institutions with a curriculum incorporating community service as a method of learning; and

International in scope and regional in application, defined by the climatic conditions of arid lands and the geography of the Greater Southwest

Preservation Studies is supported by interdisciplinary faculty from many programs at the University of Arizona including Arid Lands Studies, Anthropology, Renewable and Natural Resources, History, Art History, and Materials Sciences as well as research facilities including the Arizona State Museum, the Environmental Research Laboratory and the Materials Science Testing Laboratory. Tucson is also home to a number of regional and national research facilities critical to preservation, including the National Park Service's Western Archeological and Conservation Center (WACC), Bureau of Land Management, US Forest Service, and the Sonoran Institute, as well as municipal, regional, and state governmental agencies. Throughout the curriculum, service-learning opportunities with these and other institutions provide students real-world experience in the complexities of navigating this inter-institutional professional environment.

Cooperative Ecosystem Studies Unit (CESU)

In 2000, the University of Arizona was selected by the National Park Service as the regional host of an inter-agency Cooperative Ecosystem Studies Unit (CESU). The purpose of the CESU is to integrate the cultural and natural resource needs of a number of federal agencies – spearheaded by the National Park Service – with the technical expertise available from university-based faculty and students through funded projects. The University of Arizona's Preservation Studies has benefitted greatly from this collaborative partnership providing para-professional expertise in over 20 projects for Vanishing Treasures and other parks in both the Desert Southwest and Colorado Plateau CESUs. These parks include Organ Pipe Cactus, Salinas Pueblo Missions, Walnut Canyon, El Malpais, Chiricahua, and Casa Grande Ruins, National Monuments; Grand Canyon, Mesa Verde, Saguaro, Zion, Bryce Canyon, and Petrified Forest National Parks; and Tumacacori, Pecos, and San Antonio Missions National Historical Parks; and the Intermountain Regional Office based in Santa Fe.

Through service-learning courses, design studios, and summer team projects, as well as independent thesis and capstone research projects, the Preservation Studies curriculum provides field school-type opportunities for students to work on a number of project types including historic structures reports, building rehabilitation, National Register nominations, ruins shelter design, design and maintenance guides, cultural landscape inventories and reports, and inter-park programmatic initiatives.

Missions Initiative - Heritage Without Borders

One of the inter-park programmatic initiatives that the University of Arizona's Preservation Studies program has developed and administered is the Missions Initiative, begun in 2001. The goal of the Missions Initiative is to guide the development of an international, multidisciplinary partnership for the cultural resource management of the hundreds of Spanish Colonial mission sites in the southwestern United States and northern Mexico. Representatives from the United States National Park Service (NPS) and their Mexican counterpart, the Mexican Instituto Nacional de Antropología e Historia (INAH), are collaborating to protect cultural resources and pro-

Home page of the Missions Initiative web site.

mote heritage tourism through the re-establishment of historic links among Spanish Colonial mission sites, including many Vanishing Treasures parks. This initiative has fostered cooperative partnerships between independent research organizations, academic institutions, non-profit agencies, ecclesiastic authorities, and partners in federal, state, and local governments throughout the Greater Southwest thus promoting an ethic of heritage without borders.

The specific objectives of the Missions Initiative include:

Development of multi-disciplinary scholarship, research, publications, and curricular programs focused on Spanish Colonial mission sites;

Application of appropriate documentation standards and preservation treatments to mission buildings, archeological resources, and cultural landscapes;

Application of appropriate stewardship practices, including site management, interpretation, and technical training; and

Support of economic development of mission sites and their communities through promotion of heritage tourism.

To implement these objectives, the Missions Initiative has embarked on a number of projects:

Communications. The Missions Initiative has created, and continues to develop, a bilingual web site, (www.missions.arizona.edu) that serves as a clearinghouse for the dissemination of information, publications, reports, video-based webinars, contact resources for professional services, and on-going Missions Initiative activities.

Workshops. In November 2008, the Missions Initiative sponsored a binational TICRAT (Taller Internacional de Conservación y Restauración de Arquitectura de Tierra, or International Workshop on Conservation and Restoration of Earthen Architecture), held consecutively at Tumacacori, Arizona and Pitiquito, Sonora. The TICRAT AZ|SON, as it was called, drew 50 participants including NPS and INAH craftsmen and agency officials, academics, private-sector building professionals, community participants, and students from numerous states on both sides of the border for a week-long event of lectures, case studies, tours, and, most importantly, hands-on field workshops in the areas of building assessment and stabilization, adobe brick-making, and lime plaster preparation and application. Throughout the workshop, videographers accompanied the workshop capturing the entire week's core knowledge, construction principles, and technical skills with the goal of disseminating it to a much broader audience via web-based videos and webinars in both English and Spanish available on the Missions Initiative web site. Other TICRATs are being planned, as well as other workshops on other preservation issues.

Inventory Project. The project team has recently received funding for the development of a meta-database and protocol to provide one comprehensive source for resource location, condition, management, and protection data from a variety of existing databases. The goal is to provide retrievable information in a commonly developed database with an inventory of mission sites in the American states of Texas, New Mexico, Arizona, and California, and the Mexican states of Baja California, Sonora, Chihuahua, Coahuila, Nuevo Leon, and Tamaulipas.

Preservation Best Practices. A project currently seeking funding is the development of a compendium of case studies of various mission sites to use as prototypes of preservation projects to be disseminated through the Missions Initiative web site and other

NPS Exhibit Specialist and adobe expert David Yubeta (center) is videotaped as part of a TICRAT AZ|SON workshop.
Photo: R. Brooks Jeffery

locations. Beyond just technical preservation skills, the compendium would include best practices in other thematic criteria such as site management, financial sustainability, and heritage tourism.

Observations

Working with Vanishing Treasures parks through the CESU network has produced a great number of projects and relationships. It has also provided the opportunity to reflect on these experiences with a set of observations that might guide parks and other university partners in their future projects.

Collaboration must begin before projects begin, requiring multi-agency participation and respecting that not all partnerships are equal. Like team-based decision making, the success of a project is based on an honest assessment of each team member's contribution requiring collaborative consultation in advance of project initiation. This is also true of multi-disciplinary collaboration within parks, particularly in the attempt to balance natural and cultural resource priorities.

Vanishing Treasures and the National Park Service must look outside of the agency for models of collaboration and resource stewardship as well as cooperative ventures. Resources know no jurisdictional boundaries, yet the CESU network has very little participation from federal land management agencies outside the National Park Service. Other federal, state, and municipal agencies, as well as private and non-profit cultural resource firms, could provide alternative, and sometimes more innovative, models that could be applied to the National Park Service, and vice-versa.

Funding priorities in the National Park Service are natural resource-biased. More funds for research, projects, and training must be directed to cultural resources – and specifically the Vanishing Treasures program – to sustain our nation's cultural resources for future generations. There is also a need to provide funding for more interdisciplinary projects that integrate natural and cultural resource assessment, treatment, and management so that park leadership is less burdened with making trans-disciplinary management decisions on their own.

The creation of the next generation of Vanishing Treasures per-

The Mission of Santiago y Nuestra Señora del Pilar de Cocóspera in Sonora, Mexico, one of the sites included in the Missions Initiative. Photo: R. Brooks Jeffery

sonnel requires a much stronger relationship between the National Park Service and educational institutions. Vanishing Treasures and universities are an ideal inter-agency partnership in an era of decreased funding for both federal agencies and state universities. Universities are ideal partners that can provide neutral facilitation advocacy in the stewardship of park resources and inter-park programmatic initiatives, such as the Missions Initiative. The University of Arizona's Preservation Studies program is a model for such a partnership providing interdisciplinary, para-professional educational opportunities in a service-learning environment. For their part, parks, in their transition from relying on private-sector professionals for cultural resource services to the use of the CESU network of universities and students, must also modify their expectations of professional quality deliverables with the para-professional skills that students can provide. For this partnership to be successful, the CESU network must also provide a much stronger peer network for university partners to share best practices and provide feedback to the CESU leadership with the goal of continued improvement.

Finally, there is a need for a National Center for Preservation Technology and Training (NCPTT)-type research & training center focused on specific needs of cultural resources of the arid West that corresponds to the mission of the Vanishing Treasures program. This center could be a stand-alone facility, like NCPTT, or could be aligned with a park or university with the facilities, personnel, and curricular infrastructure to support the center's mission. Universities could also provide an ideal forum for resource management education of the next-generation of technical and executive professionals in both cultural and natural resources.

R. Brooks Jeffery
Associate Dean
Coordinator, Preservation Studies
College of Architecture and Landscape Architecture
The University of Arizona
520-621-2991
rbjeffer@u.arizona.edu
http://cala.arizona.edu/preservation
www.missions.arizona.edu

Vanishing Treasures
Arizona

Mummy Cave Ruins, Canyon de Chelly National Monument

Photo: Michael Denson

◇ Canyon de Chelly National Monument ◇ Casa Grande Ruins National Monument ◇
◇ Coronado National Memorial ◇ Fort Bowie National Historic Site ◇
◇ Grand Canyon National Park ◇ Montezuma Castle National Monument ◇
◇ Navajo National Monument ◇ Organ Pipe Cactus National Monument ◇
◇ Petrified Forest National Park ◇ Saguaro National Park ◇ Tonto National Monument ◇
◇ Tumacacori National Historical Park ◇ Tuzigoot National Monument ◇
◇ Walnut Canyon National Monument ◇ Wupatki National Monument ◇

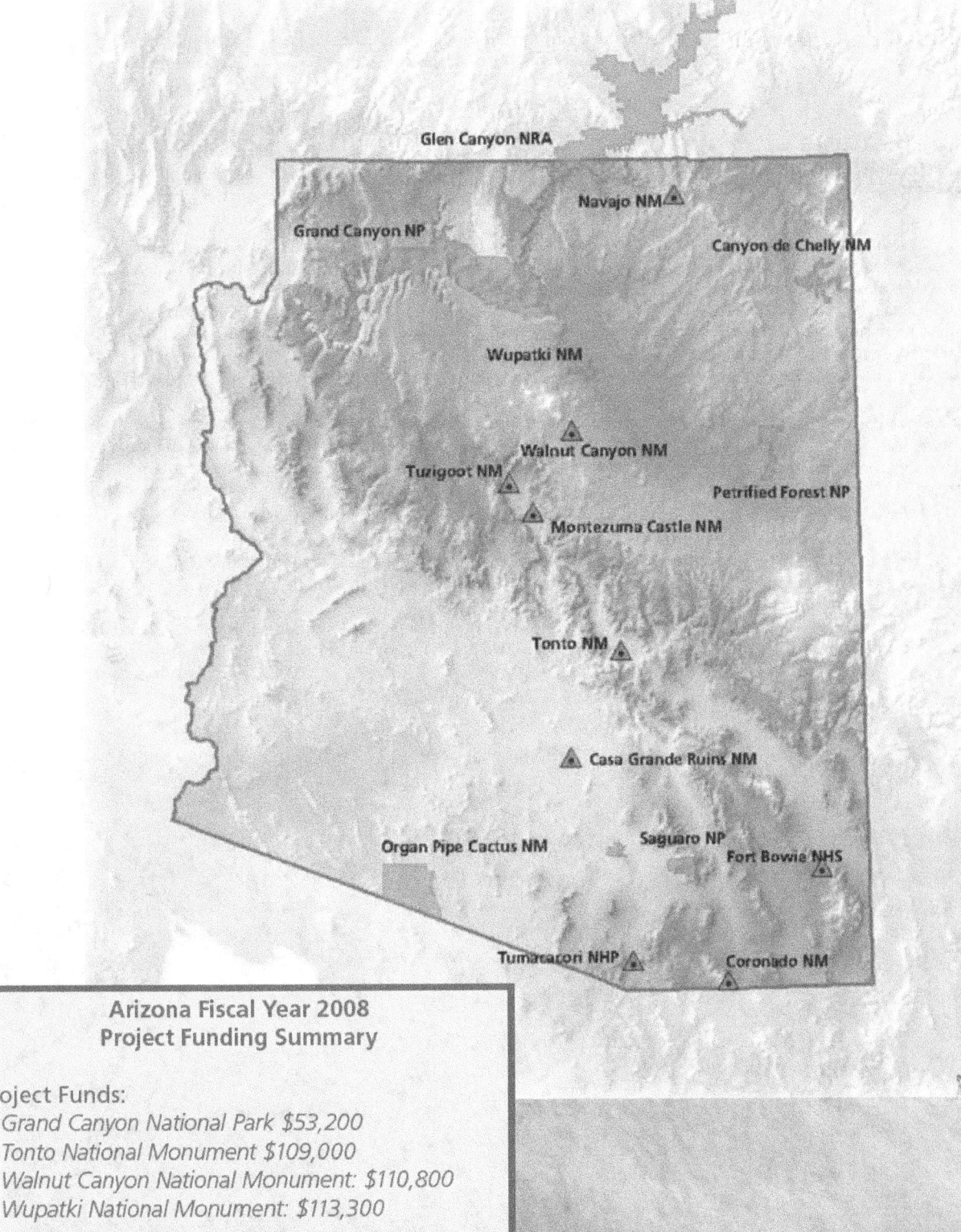

Glen Canyon NRA

Navajo NM ▲

Grand Canyon NP

Canyon de Chelly NM

Wupatki NM

Walnut Canyon NM ▲

Tuzigoot NM ▲

Petrified Forest NP

Montezuma Castle NM ▲

Tonto NM ▲

Casa Grande Ruins NM ▲

Organ Pipe Cactus NM

Saguaro NP

Fort Bowie NHS ▲

Tumacacori NHP ▲

Coronado NM ▲

N

**Arizona Fiscal Year 2008
Project Funding Summary**

Project Funds:
  Grand Canyon National Park $53,200
  Tonto National Monument $109,000
  Walnut Canyon National Monument: $110,800
  Wupatki National Monument: $113,300

Canyon de Chelly National Monument (CACH)

VANISHING TREASURES ACCOMPLISHMENTS AND CHALLENGES

VT Challenges and Successes: The biggest challenge in the management of Canyon de Chelly National Monument is balancing the needs of a living Navajo community with the needs of a sustainable and effective resource management program. In addition, the canyon's erosional environment poses a significant long-term challenge to VT resources.

Consultation: Canyon de Chelly consulted with the Navajo Nation's Historic Preservation Department on a periodic basis and has kept the tribe informed of projects and activities as they relate to park cultural resources.

Safety: In FY 2008, the Cultural Resources Division maintained an effective safety program. Job Hazard Analyses (JHAs) were developed and maintained for all projects as well as for office and front country duties.

Weekly division safety meetings were held throughout the duration of the field season.

VANISHING TREASURES STAFF

Jennifer L. Lavris, Archeologist
FY 2002 Position

Jennifer is an archeologist, specializing in North American archeology, historic architecture, human osteology, database management, digital imaging, and Egyptology. This year, Jennifer co-managed the park Cultural Resources Program with Keith Lyons (see below). Her primary duties included archeological database management; Section 106/110 compliance; Native American Graves Repatriation and Protection Act (NAGPRA) compliance, archeological site monitoring, the development of project and research designs, and the management of the program's budget.

Jennifer served as the database manager for the Watershed Project Archeological Survey (WPAS), DeHarport Archeological Site Relocation Survey (DASRS), Archeological Site Management Information System-Corrective Action Plan (ASMIS-CAP 2008), and Control Point Network projects. In that capacity she supervised two base-funded full-

time term archeological technicians (GS-5) over a field season that began in April and continued through October, 2008. Concurrently she was responsible for the processing of data and the management of information collected in the current and in previous years. The Control Point Network project was designed by Jennifer in 2008 and was funded through a Western National Parks Association (WNPA) grant.

Jennifer also continued work on the division's digital imaging project, which is digitizing all historic park photography, the color slides and black and white prints from the 1990s Archeological Preservation Project (APP), and the 1940s David DeHarport archeological survey photos. To date, over 5,000 images have been digitized, with all digitized photographs correctly renamed and organized into an image database. The database will be cataloged and will be searchable by keywords.

Training: Jennifer completed instructor-led training with the Topcon GPT-9003A robotic total station, Topcon static/RTK GR-3 GNSS (multi-constellation) system, and the handheld Topcon GMS 2 data collection system.

Cultural Resource Management crew setting up a control point network along the North Rim using Holman's Topcon surveying equipment.
Photo: Michael Denson

**Keith D. Lyons,
Archeologist
FY 2003 Position**

Keith is an archeologist, specializing in North American archeology, site preservation, cultural landscapes, human osteology, and archival management. In FY 2008, Keith along with Jennifer Lavris, co-managed the park Cultural Resources Program. His primary duties included archeological site monitoring, field supervision, Section 106/110 and NAGPRA compliance, archeological survey and overall program development. Keith also continued to manage park collections this past year, which included managing the park museum and database. Keith served as the field supervisor for the WPAS, DASRS, ASMIS-CAP 2008, and Control Point Network projects. In that capacity he supervised two base-funded full-time term archeological technicians (GS-5) through a field season that began in April and continued through October, 2008.

Keith continued to design the park archival

*Holly Johanns recording site conditions at Mummy Cave Ruins.
Photo: Michael Denson*

inventory project, which aims to generate an accurate report of the park's scientific archives. This inventory will include all archeological site files, bound and unbound; site and stabilization reports; photography; and maps. Keith is also responsible for entering park projects into the Planning, Environment, and Public Comment (PEPC) database/web site. In FY 2008, he also became the Park Research Coordinator, where

he facilitates a broad range of park research that includes both cultural and natural resources.

In November, Keith presented an update of ongoing park archeological projects during the park's Annual Guides Training.

Training: In FY 2008, Keith completed instructor-led training with the TOPCON GPT-9003A robotic total station, Topcon static/RTK GR-3 GNSS (multi-constellation) system, and the handheld Topcon GMS 2 data collection system. He also attended PEPC Training held at Petrified Forest National Park and he completed the Telnet course entitled "Ethics for New Supervisors."

VANISHING TREASURES PROJECT FUNDING

Canyon de Chelly National Monument did not receive project funding this year.

Casa Grande Ruins National Monument (CAGR)

VANISHING TREASURES ACCOMPLISHMENTS AND CHALLENGES

VT Challenges and Successes: Casa Grande Ruins National Monument's highest priority for resource protection and ruins preservation is to ensure that all of the exposed archeological features are fully documented and protected from accelerating deterioration resulting from previous disturbances, poor site drainage, differential fill erosion, and animal interactions.

Our greatest success is attributable to the help of special projects funding that has allowed us to significantly expand the Resources Division. In 2008, the division included one permanent, one term, and three

*The Big House at dusk, Casa Grande Ruins National Monument.
Photo: Jim Creager*

seasonal staff, plus several volunteers. With this enhanced staffing, we have begun to compile site histories, draft site preservation plans, and enhance our consultation with Native American tribes. We are also implementing recommendations for documentation, updating condition assessment, continuing our monitoring program, and implementing recommended preservation treatments. We also drafted a preservation plan for Compound B that includes a thorough history of an earlier site study, as well as the excavation and stabilization of the site. Consultation and review of this plan has been initiated. Resources staff and volunteers reviewed all of the uncataloged files and maps from the monument's library and staff offices. All of the maps were digitally scanned and transferred to the Western Archeological and Conservation Center (WACC) for long-term curation. The ruins stabilization records and other documents relating to the construction, renovation, or preservation of historic structures were inventoried and itemized according to location and task before inclusion in the updated central administrative filing system at Casa Grande. The digitized maps and inventoried files have been an essential reference tool for resource management planning efforts in 2008.

Emergency fill level restoration was conducted at five archeological sites within the park in 2008, and an active hive of bees was removed from a structural crack in the north exterior wall of the Great House. Through money from the Federal Lands Recreation and Enhancement Act (FLREA), we initiated a 3-D documentation project for the archeological features at publicly accessible archeological sites in the park, and this high level of documentation will continue with additional funding from the Vanishing Treasures Program in 2009.

Consultation: During consultation meetings, two suggestions were made by our affiliated tribes and both have become the subject of new funding proposals. One suggestion resulted in a funding proposal to the National Park Foundation for $9,965 to conduct a workshop with park rangers and culturally affiliated tribes to improve the interpretation of cultural resources at Casa Grande Ruins National Monument. The second resulted in an application to the Native American Graves Protection and Repatriation Act (NAGPRA) FY 2009 Internship Program to facilitate cooperation with our culturally affiliated tribes on ethnographic consultations relating to the proposed Visitor Center Expansion Project.

Stabilization work on Compound A, Casa Grande Ruins National Monument. Photo: Courtesy Casa Grande Ruins National Monument

Safety: The predominant safety-related challenge for monument staff is reaching the upper levels of the Great House and the Ruins Shelter for monitoring and maintenance tasks. Occupational Safety and Health Administration (OSHA) scaffolding regulations assume different site conditions than those found at Casa Grande; nevertheless, safety requirements mandate that contractors and staff comply with OSHA regulations. A Monument goal is to acquire scaffolding training to accommodate our unique conditions and meet OSHA requirements.

VANISHING TREASURES STAFF

Rebecca Carr, Archeologist
FY 2001 Position

This position was originally filled as an Exhibit Specialist. When Larry Stewart accepted the position of Chief of Maintenance in 2004, it was converted to an Archeologist and Rebecca was hired to fill the vacancy in FY 2005.

In FY 2008, Rebecca supervised the resource staff and oversaw all of the park's cultural resource projects as well as its integrated pest management program. As an important component of resource management projects this year, Native American consultation resulted in increased dialog between members of the park's culturally affiliated tribes and park staff.

Rebecca made two presentations at the Intermountain Region Resource Stewardship Conference; one on the historic use of plaster amendments at Casa Grande and its implications for cultural resource management today, and another that focused on Integrated Pest Management research at the park. Rebecca was also invited to make a

presentation at the Seminario Internacional de Conservacion y Restauracion de Architectura de Tierra (SICRAT) sponsored by the Instituto Nacional de Antropología e Historia (INAH) at Paquimé in Casas Grandes, Chihuahua, Mexico, and she hosted provincial monument directors from Afghanistan as a participant in a training and exchange program sponsored by the State Department and the George Wright Society.

Rebecca was also the Intermountain Region recipient of the Appelman-Judd-Lewis Award for Resource Management.

Rebecca specializes in condition assessment, preservation, and resource management for earthen and masonry architecture, and she has experience applying conservation treatments to earthen murals. She has also worked with historic mining structures, and performed community outreach, non-profit management, and museum collections activities within historic mining communities. She has formal training in integrated pest management (IPM) for historic structures and archeological sites and is licensed by the State of Arizona Structural Pest Control Commission as a pesticide applicator.

Training: Rebecca participated in a full week of safety training, Museum Management Training, and ANCS+ museum and archival collections management software training in FY 2008.

VANISHING TREASURES PROJECT FUNDING

Casa Grande Ruins National Monument did not receive project funding this year.

Flagstaff Area National Monuments (FLAG)

The Flagstaff Area Monuments are comprised of Wupatki (WUPA), Sunset Crater Volcano (SUCR), and Walnut Canyon (WACA) National Monuments

VANISHING TREASURES ACCOMPLISHMENTS AND CHALLENGES

VT Challenges and Successes: Our main challenge this year was obtaining an access route to a backcountry project site and completing the compliance needed to do so. A route was needed to get backfill material to the site, and the most expedient way was through motorized means. Once we had worked our way through the wilderness compliance process, getting the work done was relatively easy. We were able to save from imminent collapse three rooms that had been excavated in the 1960s to a depth below floor level, leaving the basal stones exposed. The successful completion of this project was a major achievement for the park.

Consultation: No consultation-related problems were encountered.

Safety: A utility vehicle (UTV) was safely used to move a considerable quantity of backfill material to our project site, which was located about half a mile from the staging area.

VANISHING TREASURES STAFF

Lloyd Masayumptewa, Archeologist FY 1998 Position

Lloyd was hired in May 2007 to fill the Supervisory Archeologist position that Al Remley vacated in August 2006. With Al Remley's, Lyle Balenquah's and Ian Hough's positions remaining vacant into FY 2008, he was actively involved in a number of preservation projects and assignments related to VT resources including work at both Wupatki (WUPA) and Walnut Canyon (WACA) National Monuments. Lloyd was responsible for implementing and contracting all preservation activities in both parks with assistance from his crew. He and his preservation crew successfully completed five Cultural Cyclic projects and two VT projects, and they initiated a CRPP-Base inventory project at Sunset Crater National Monument.

In addition, Lloyd has had responsibility for writing work plans; writing project proposals; closing out the Archeology Program's budget; writing completion reports for FY 2008 projects; submitting the FLAG Archeological Site Management Information System (ASMIS) data and superintendent's certification; conducting employee appraisals; and overseeing the day-to-day operation of the archeology crews.

Lisa Baldwin, Archeologist FY 1999 Position

In FY 2008, Lisa was actively involved in a number of preservation projects and assignments related to VT resources including work at both Wupatki and Walnut Canyon

National Monuments. With Lyle Balenquah's and Ian Hough's positions remaining vacant through FY 2008 (see below), Lisa has taken the lead on some preservation activities in both parks and she has successfully directed the implementation of a number of field projects.

Archeologist FY 2000 Position (Vacant)

This position, previously filled by Lyle Balenquah, was vacant for all of FY 2008. Lapse salary was used for other park needs.

Archeologist FY 2003 Position (Vacant)

This position, previously filled by Ian Hough, was vacant for all of FY 2008. Lapse salary was used for other park needs.

John Cannella, Geographer/ Geographical Information System (GIS) Specialist FY 2004 Position (TERM converted to Permanent)

John was hired in May, 2004, to fill the Flagstaff Area National Monuments GIS/Database Management position, a unique position that is jointly funded by the VT Program and the Natural Resource Challenge Program. His position was converted to a permanent position during FY 2007.

In FY 2008, John was responsible for overall GIS and Data Management for FLAG, including administration of park cultural databases and GIS data sets. He worked on developing cultural resource GIS data sets, including site datums, site boundary,

Panoramic view from the Citadel, Wupatki National Monument.
Photo: Randall Skeirik

Preservation crew member TJ tamping fill in Antelope House, Wupatki National Monument.
Photo: Courtesy Wupatki National Monument.

site feature, and isolated occurrence layers with metadata for each of the Flagstaff Area Monuments. With the help of Cultural Resource staff, John also implemented a flexible information management system to store and retrieve digital site files, maps, and images from GIS. He also provided ongoing GIS/GPS support and training for FLAG Cultural Resource staff.

In addition, John has developed and implemented an agreement to provide GIS services to three National Monuments in northern Arizona (Tonto, Montezuma Castle, and Tuzigoot) that will mine existing data and create metadata and data management directory structures that conform to Intermountain Region guidelines. This has proven to be a highly successful partnership because of both a strong emphasis on communication between parks and the ability to select outstanding GIS talent from Northern Arizona University's (NAU) GIS certificate program.

VANISHING TREASURES PROJECT FUNDING

Walnut Canyon National Monument

Project Name: Architectural Condition Assessment of Fifth Fort

Project Summary: Within the Monument boundaries are five fort sites for which FLAG has been attempting to derive more defined information. In FY 2008, funding that was originally intended for the Fifth Fort Complex (a project that was completed ahead of schedule last year) was applied to a project to complete the Fourth Fort Complex (which is slated to receive funding in FY 2009). Because of property ownership problems with the Second Fort Complex (part of the site is outside park boundaries), we have revised our project schedule with VT Leadership Committee approval to provide time to negotiate an agreement with the in-holder. Thanks to this flexibility on the part of the of the VT Chair and

Leadership, we have been able to complete the documentation of four of the five Fort Complexes, and we hope to complete a condition assessment on some or all of the Second Fort Complex in FY 2009.

The Fourth Fort Complex project involved conducting formal condition assessments and documentation on ten architectural cliff dwelling sites (WACA 10-11 and 210-217). These ten sites, located in the eastern section of Walnut Canyon National Monument, date to the Elden Phase (A.D. 1125-1250) of the Sinagua Culture. Although these sites were recorded as part of an archeological survey of Walnut Canyon National Monument in 1985, the information was too general for use in long-term preservation planning and mitigation. The maps and photos that were created were not comprehensive and did not capture necessary information on the condition of the Fourth Fort sites. Furthermore, many of the sites have been the subjected to a policy of benign neglect

Backfill is placed in selected rooms at Antelope House, Wupatki National Monument. Photo: Courtesy Wupatki National Monument.

for a number of years and have never been documented, assessed, or treated.

Project Budget: $110,800

Personnel:	$29,476
Vehicles:	$0
Travel/Training:	$2,155
Supplies/Materials:	$2,120
Equipment:	$0
Services/Contracts:	$21,401
Other:	$55,648

Project Accomplishments: This project addressed the lack of information on the integrity (amount of original intact architecture remaining), condition (stability, types and rate of deterioration, threats); and proposed preservation treatments needed at each site to keep the architecture in a good, safe, and stable condition. The data collected during this project will be used to identify areas in need of treatment, to develop effective preservation plans, and establish a schedule, if necessary, for cyclic preservation maintenance. In addition, the information will provide baseline data for long-term monitoring to determine if, and at what rate, architectural fabric is being lost or altered as a result of environmental processes or human activity.

The project was a collaborative undertaking between the National Park Service and Northern Arizona University via a cooperative agreement under the Colorado Plateau Cooperative Ecosystem Study Unit (CP-

CESU). Working together with our staff of term and seasonal archeologists, the university students produced planimetric maps (plan views, wall elevations, and cross sections) and documentation photography (scaled black-and-white prints and color slides), and they filled out tabular condition assessments forms. A final report will be produced that summarizes the condition of the sites and provides recommendations for future preservation treatments.

VANISHING TREASURES PROJECT FUNDING

Wupatki National Monument

Project Name: Perform Emergency Treatment/Repairs for Antelope House Pueblo

Project Summary: Antelope House, located in the Wupatki Basin, was first recorded by Harold Colton of the Museum of Northern Arizona in 1932. The Park Service, under the direction of Charles Voll and Martin Mayer, excavated and stabilized Antelope House in 1965. The artifact assemblage indicates a possible AD 1100-1250 occupation by Ancestral Puebloan peoples.

Excavated in 1965, Antelope House, an eight-room pueblo with two detached structures and four wing walls, had been left untreated and exposed to the elements for over 40 years. Continued exposure would have soon resulted in the collapse of several rooms. This project involved conducting

emergency stabilization and backfilling of the site.

Project Budget: $113,300

Personnel:	$27,130
Vehicles:	$1,425
Travel/Training:	$1,691
Supplies/Materials:	$6,122
Equipment:	$1,461
Services/Contracts:	$74,956
Other:	$216

Project Accomplishments: Antelope House was extensively documented beginning in 1987 when it was re-recorded as part of the Wupatki Survey. Planimetric maps, architectural documentation, and condition assessments were completed in 2001. Prior to the implementation of this project, aerial photographs and a topographic map of the area around Antelope House were initiated under contract with Western Mapping, Inc.

The project consisted of backfilling three of the rooms (1, 2, and 8) that were excavated in 1965. Because the site had been left exposed since the 1965 excavation project, continued deterioration of the exposed flooring and footings posed a risk to the remaining architecture, which averaged 2 meters high in the three rooms slated for backfilling.

The rooms were first cleaned of any vegetation and then lined with geotextile to differentiate original material from backfill. Sterile fill, ranging from 25 to 50 cm, was added to protect exposed original fabric. The fill was contoured to allow water to drain into the center of the rooms and away from standing walls. A total of 3,450 gallons of fill were added to the three rooms.

The fill was transported from the New Heiser Maintenance yard by a pick-up truck pulling a hydraulic dump trailer using a well-established dirt road. The fill was deposited at a staging area ½ mile down from Antelope House, where it was transferred by a Bobcat to the UTV for transport up to Antelope House. The route taken by the UTV followed alluvial washes and a route established during the 1965 excavation and stabilization project. The fill was stockpiled at a second staging area near the pueblo and hauled by wheelbarrow and buckets to the rooms. The UTV trail and staging areas were rehabilitated at the end of the project.

In addition, some minor stabilization work was done in the form of repointing mortar joints, filling holes and voids, and resetting capstones. All the work performed during this project will be documented in a completion report.

Fort Bowie National Historic Site (FOBO)

VANISHING TREASURES ACCOMPLISHMENTS AND CHALLENGES

VT Challenges and Successes: This year, our stabilization crew concentrated on repairing Fort Bowie's water reservoirs. Work was completed on four water reservoirs: the Main Reservoir (LSC14086), Reservoir (LCS14085), Reservoir (LCS14088), and the Indian Agency Reservoir (LCS14122). Three of the reservoirs were located off the trail and were harder to access than most other structures. Materials and equipment had to be hauled to these remote sites on an ATV and great care was taken to avoid damage to the area surrounding the sites.

The reservoir work was accomplished ahead of schedule, allowing us to turn our attention to four foundations that were listed in poor condition on the List of Classified Structures (LCS). These structures included Earth Closet (LCS14071), Earth Closet (LCS14073), Fire Hydrant Foundation (LCS14065), and a Stone Retaining Wall (LCS14108) at the First Fort. As a result, these foundations have now been returned to good condition.

Safety: Safety considerations remained the same as in previous years: sun, heat, wasps, and snakes. This year, however, several of the structures we were working on were a

The Second Fort, Fort Bowie National Historic Site.
Photo: Courtesy Fort Bowie National Historic Site

considerable distance from roads or trails. Materials for stabilization were hauled to the site in wheelbarrows or on ATVs, requiring considerable attention to the terrain around each site. Utilizing proper footing and lifting techniques, no injuries were incurred.

VANISHING TREASURES STAFF

Fernie Nunez, Masonry Worker
FY 1998 Position

Fernie and the stabilization crew had an exceptional year in FY 2008. Not only were they able to complete the stabilization of four large reservoirs well ahead of schedule,

they also made repairs to four other structures that were listed in poor condition on the LCS. These were the last four structures in poor condition on the list, fully satisfying Government Performance and Results Act (GPRA) goal Ia5-Historic Structures (LCS) to bring 100% of the park's historic structures on the current List of Classified Structures into good condition. With completion of treatment to these four structures, emphasis can now shift to routine maintenance that will ensure that all of the park's LCS structures remain in good condition.

Fernie is skilled in adobe work, plastering, and rock pointing. He is also good with small engines and maintaining equipment in good operating condition.

Phil Tapia, Masonry Worker
FY 1999 Position

Accomplishments: As lead person of the stabilization crew, Phil procured materials scheduled for stabilization work, documented techniques used, and assisted the crew with the field work. Under his direction, four reservoirs were repaired and four additional structures were brought from poor to good condition.

Phil is very good with adobe work, plastering, and rock pointing. He is the lead person for our annual ruins stabilization projects, monitoring and documenting the work performed.

VANISHING TREASURES PROJECT FUNDING

Fort Bowie National Historical Site did not receive project funding this year.

Seasonal maintenance worker Ethan Mower and Fernie Nunez plastering a reservoir at Fort Bowie National Historic Site.
Photo: Courtesy Fort Bowie National Historic Site

Grand Canyon National Park (GRCA)

VANISHING TREASURES ACCOMPLISHMENTS AND CHALLENGES

Consultation: Grand Canyon Vanishing Treasures staff successfully consulted on two occasions with the Navajo Nation for work on historic wooden structures and also consulted with our other 11 affiliated Native America tribes and the Arizona State Historic Preservation Office (AZSHPO) on a ruins stabilization project at the Transept Ruin site.

Safety: Over the course of a 45 day field season, the Grand Canyon Vanishing Treasures crew completed both a condition assessment project in the Deer Creek and Tapeats Creek drainages and other ruins preservation activities while successfully maintaining employee safety. Job Hazard Analyses (JHAs), hazardous risk assessments, and safety walk-around procedures were written for both field and lab activities. Safety issues were discussed with the crew to foster an attitude of "safety first", resulting in no lost-time injuries for VT personnel. The seasonal field crew also attended a one-day backcountry safety workshop hosted by staff of the park's Division of Visitor and Resource Protection.

VANISHING TREASURES STAFF

Ellen Brennan, Lead Vanishing Treasures Archeologist
FY 2000 Position

Ellen served as the contracting officer's representative (COR) on the Clear Creek mapping project, completing a VT mapping effort that was initiated in 1999. During this project, a new site locus and new features were identified, mapped, and recorded. Both a series of maps and a technical mapping report were produced.

Additionally, Ellen participated in the Grand Canyon Archeological Project, excavating and recording architectural features at the Palisades site. She also conducted VT condition assessments on a group of sites along the North Kaibab trail, assisting with site condition assessments for the Archeological Sites Management Information System (ASMIS), assisted with the preservation work at the Transept ruin, and assisted with routine preservation housekeeping at Tusayan Ruin.

Ellen co-led a survey project in the Pasture Wash area as part of a week-long Grand Canyon Field Institute hands-on archeology class; she participated as part of a team that developed a new interpretive display for the Bright Angel Pueblo; and she was the project leader for the September Colorado River Management Plan monitoring project. Along with Steven Schooler, Ellen monitored 59 sites and recorded one new site during the 18-day trip; and she planned treatment activities at several high use areas along the Colorado River.

Ellen was a presenter at the Intermountain Region Resource Stewardship Conference in May, 2008. She also directed data recovery activities at an archeology site in the Hermit's Rest area in advance of

the placement of a septic system and later completed the preliminary report on the Hermit Septic data recovery findings as well as the architectural findings of the Furnace Flat excavation that took place at the end of 2007.

Ellen is skilled in condition assessment, architectural documentation, analysis of data collection activities, form and manual development, digital cartography, graphic illustration, AutoCAD, Illustrator, GIS, and database development. She specializes in archeology applications for digital cartographic and architectural illustration using AutoCAD and Illustrator; GIS development and use; database development related to recording architectural features; review of data forms and data collection practices to improve retrieval and analysis of data for research-based syntheses; development of procedures manuals and stabilization histories; development and use of data collection techniques such as DNR Garmin, Pathfinder Office, and associated data collectors.

Training: Ellen attended a mortar workshop conducted at Casa Grande National Monument and attended many informative workshops during the IMR Conference for Comprehensive Resource Stewardship.

Ian Hough, Vanishing Treasures Archeologist
FY 2005 Position

Ian completed Vanishing Treasures stabilization, condition assessment, and architectural documentation projects at

Sunrise on the Esplanade, Grand Canyon National Park.
Photo: Frank Romaglia

Seasonal archeologist Margie Shaw documents a granary.
Photo: Courtesy Grand Canyon National Park.

seven sites including Bright Angel Ruin, Tusayan Ruin, Transept Ruin, Tapeats Creek, Deer Creek, Thunder River Trail, and Zuni Point historic Native American structures.

He participated in the Grand Canyon Archeology Project conducted at the Ivo site on the Colorado River, where he completed feature excavations and conducted architectural documentation and condition assessments. He also designed a research project for architectural earthen mortars for this project.

Ian continued testing stabilization material for Tusayan Ruin, Kiva A. Through this testing, the all-organic Stabilizer Solutions product has been selected as the preferred material for stabilizing the Kiva bench cap in 2009.

Ian also participated in the Intermountain Region Resource Stewardship Conference in May in Tucson, AZ, where he presented results of the 2006 3-D scanning and documentation of historic Native American wooden structures. He also made a presentation on the testing of stabilization materials at Grand Canyon at the preservation materials testing workshop at Casa Grande NM.

Ian has specialized in the areas of historic Native American wooden structures, GPS data collection, and Stabilizer Solution material application. He is skilled in remote-area VT project planning; condition assessment; architectural documentation methods for Puebloan, historic Native American and Historic Euro-American structures; digital cartography; graphic illustration;

AutoCAD, Illustrator, Trimble GPS and GIS software; and database development.

VANISHING TREASURES PROJECT FUNDING

Project Name: Complete Condition Assessments of Architectural Sites in the Deer Creek and Tapeats Creek Drainages

PMIS Number: 115236

Project Summary: The project involved completing condition assessments for architectural sites located in the Deer Creek and Tapeats Creek drainages in the Grand Canyon backcountry.

Project Budget: $53,200.00

Personnel:	$31,886.60
Vehicles:	$2,551.13
Travel/Training:	$1,934.31
Supplies/Materials:	$4353.96
Equipment:	$584
Services/Contracts:	$11,890.00
Other:	$0

Project Accomplishments: This project was designed to collect baseline condition information on architectural remains and assess preservation needs at 11 archeology sites containing 44 individual structures in the Tapeats and Deer Creek drainages at Grand Canyon National Park. All sites were selected for their exceptionally well-preserved architecture and their proximity to areas with high visitor use that have impacted archeology sites in the past. Fieldwork for the project was completed in FY 2008 with project tasks (both fieldwork and office) conducted by Grand Canyon National Park Archeology (Vanishing Treasures) staff including Ellen Brennan, Ian Hough, Margaret Shaw and Tom Fuller. Because of the strenuous nature of the

site access, this project did not involve volunteers and no services were received from outside parties.

Project goals were met, and exceeded, by collecting new and updated site information (site descriptions, photographs, site maps and global positioning system coordinates). Of the 11 sites investigated, nine were found to be in good condition, one in fair condition, and one in poor condition.

The 44 structures documented included 23 nearly complete granary rooms and 21 open-air coursed masonry structures. All but 4 of the granaries are either completely or partially intact and stable. The remaining four are unstable; and gradual, natural collapse is likely. The well preserved granaries all contained original masonry of stone and mortar materials. Two of the open air-structures studied are collapsed, while the remaining 19 are partially or completely intact and stable. Although each room and structure showed signs of varying degrees of impact from exposure to natural erosion, none will require physical treatment in the next 5 years to slow or stop these impacts. The greatest threats to the original architecture are visitor overuse and vandalism, both of which are to be addressed with frequent monitoring and law enforcement patrols.

In addition to the Deer and Tapeats Creek sites, three large stabilized architectural sites (Transept Ruin, Bright Angel Ruin, and Tusayan Ruin, all of which are open for public interpretation) received stabilization maintenance with funding and personnel from this project. Prior to the 2008 stabilization maintenance, Transept Ruin was badly degraded and unstable; Bright Angel Ruin was overgrown with thick vegetation and needed drainage improvements; and one structure at Tusayan Ruin was in poor condition, due to weathering of a previously stabilized feature. These three small-scale housekeeping-type projects served as training for the seasonal Vanishing Treasures crew and all three sites are now in good condition. The total cost of the project was $53,200.00, all of which was obligated in FY 2008.

Five additional sites in Deer Creek will be examined during the fall of 2008 and spring of 2009. The estimated time needed to complete the remainder of the project is two weeks. Once the project is complete, a technical report of the project will be prepared and published on the park's web site.

Montezuma Castle and Tuzigoot National Monuments (MOCA/TUZI)

VANISHING TREASURES STAFF

John Schroeder, Archeologist
FY 1999 Position, Converted in FY 2004

John started at Tuzigoot as a Student Temporary Employee Program (STEP) archeological technician in February, 2004. In 2005, after the retirement of one of our VT masons, the position was converted to an archeologist, and John was moved into that position as a Student Career Experience Program (SCEP) archeologist. John served in that position until May of 2008 when he left to take a position at Joshua Tree National Park.

Prior to his departure, John continued to oversee the completion of the stabilization of a series of 19 cavates located at Montezuma Castle National Monument and the publication of a narrative report outlining previous work, current conditions, and recommendations for stabilization treatments. The cavate stabilization followed last year's project that generated metrically scaled plan view maps and AutoCAD elevation drawings, medium-format photographs of all architecture, and research into previous stabilization work—all of which were incorporated into the final report. The cavate project was particularly interesting because the features had never been historically stabilized and retained

Maintenance Chief Bill Osterhaus and Archeologist Matt Guebard inspect the interior of Montezuma Castle.
Photo: Randall Skeirik

intact masonry walls, plastered floor surfaces, fire pits, storage cists, and wall and ceiling plaster.

FY 2008 saw processing of the data collected in FY 2007 for the documentation of Montezuma Castle using 3D light detection and ranging (LiDAR) scanning. The the final images will be delivered in FY 2009.

The multi-year project at Tuzigoot Pueblo continued with the documentation work now more than 80% complete and approximately 70% of the stabilization work completed.

Preparations were made this year for the documentation and stabilization of a number of outlying sites at Montezuma Well, a detached unit of Montezuma Castle that is centered around a spring-fed limestone sinkhole. Although John left at the beginning of the field season, archeological technician Josh Kleinman was able to continue preparations for this project with minimal supervision. Josh was also instrumental in keeping archeological work moving forward during the time needed to refill John's position.

One month before the end of the fiscal year, we hired Matthew Guebard to fill the vacant archeologist position. Matt arrived ready to hit the ground running and immediately began to sort through files and

get acquainted with the park's resources and our pending and ongoing projects. We expect to see many accomplishments listed in the next VT *Annual Report* after Matt has had a full year on-the-job.

Matt will also serve as the park's compliance coordinator, GIS specialist, collections manager, and research coordinator.

Stefan Sloper, Masonry Worker
FY 1999 Position, Converted to Term, Subject-to-Furlough in FY 2006

VT masonry worker Alex Contreras retired in June, 2006 and his position remained vacant through most of FY 2007. Late in FY 2007 the position was advertised as a term preservation mason and was awarded to Stefan Sloper who started early in FY 2008.

Previously, Stefan had worked with Alex in a seasonal position on the stabilization of Tuzigoot pueblo.

As in previous years, Stefan removed inappropriate pointing mortars and replaced them with a softer soil/cement mix that will help to preserve the remaining historic fabric of the pueblo.

VANISHING TREASURES PROJECT FUNDING

Montezuma Castle and Tuzigoot National Monuments did not receive project funding this year.

Tuzigoot Pueblo
Photo: Randall Skeirik

Navajo National Monument (NAVA)

VANISHING TREASURES ACCOMPLISHMENTS AND CHALLENGES

VT Challenges and Successes: Despite the departure of the park archeologist part-way through the year, the crew continued to make progress on the Keet Seel stabilization history.

Safety: The crew completed FY 2008 with no lost-time injuries.

VANISHING TREASURES STAFF

**Brian Culpepper,
Archeologist
FY 2000 Position**

This position was vacant during part of FY 2008. Lapse salary was used for emergency midden recovery from the Inscription House site.

Brian spent much of the year managing the Monument's VT program, overseeing both the continued development of the Keet Seel stabilization history that was begun by Kenny Accord and the day-to-day needs of the monument as related to the Cultural Resource Division. Brian left Navajo National Monument in April 2008 to work for the Bureau of Land Management at the Agua Fria National Monument.

Brain is skilled in program management and ruins preservation.

**Jim Dryer, Archeology Technician
FY 2005 Position**

This position was originally filled as a Masonry Worker but has been converted to an Archeology Technician.

In FY 2008, Jim completed the Report: "NAVA Administrative Unit Archeological Inventory" and he presented the historical aspects of his research at the Pecos Conference in Flagstaff this past summer.

Jim also began creating a Geo-database

for the Monument, changing many of the Cultural Resource Division's geographical information systems (GIS) layers from the North American Datum of 1927 (NAD27) to the North American Datum of 1983 (NAD83); and he has produced maps for various projects. He completed the FY 2008 Archeological Sites Management Information System (ASMIS) condition assessments

*Waterfall in Betatakin Canyon, Navajo National Monument.
Photo: Courtesy Navajo National Monument*

of sites within the monument and was responsible for all ASMIS and Government Performance Results Act (GPRA) reporting.

He took the lead in the project for emergency midden recovery at the Inscription House site, and he conducted Section 106

monitoring and mitigation activities related to other park projects and maintenance activities. He was also the monument liaison for project planning and development for the removal of invasive flora such as Russian olive, tamarisk, and cheat grass.

Jim worked to determine where future preservation treatment should occur at Betatakin and where data loggers might be placed within the ruin to track environmental impacts to the architectural features of the site.

After Brian Culpepper's departure in May, Jim served as the acting park archeologist for the remainder of the fiscal year.

Jim is skilled in the use of global positioning systems (GPS) and GIS technologies and in photography.

Training: Jim received training in ArcGIS 9.2.

**Theodore Roberts,
Archeology Technician
FY 1999 Position**

This position was originally filled as an Archeologist but has been converted to an Archeology Technician.

The position was vacant during part of FY 2008 with lapsed salary going toward miscellaneous supplies and equipment.

Ted continued to work on the stabilization history of Keet Seel and he assisted with the emergency midden recovery project from Inscription House where he wrote the scope of work and developed the Cooperative Ecosystem Study Unit (CESU) agreement through which the project was executed. Ted left Navajo National Monument in August, 2008 to work as an archeologist in the private sector in Flagstaff, AZ.

VANISHING TREASURES PROJECT FUNDING

Navajo National Monument did not receive project funding this year.

Organ Pipe National Monument (ORPI)

VANISHING TREASURES ACCOMPLISHMENTS AND CHALLENGES

VT Challenges and Successes: "Monumental" is the most fitting description for the challenges facing Vanishing Treasures preservation efforts at Organ Pipe Cactus National Monument in 2009. The VT archeologist position was vacant for much of 2008 after Joseph Tuomey left for a job with the Bureau of Land Management. Many of the park's historic resources, including historic cattle ranches such as Dos Lomitas and Bates Well Ranch, their associated line camps, and features such as "sandwich-style" corral fences, desert coolers, and uniquely constructed ramadas are in urgent need of stabilization, restoration, or repair. These "southwestern" and Sonoran Desert-style historic ranching features are part of the cultural resources for which the Monument was created and are deteriorating alarmingly. In addition, ORPI has over 90 historic gold, silver, and copper mines, some of which are listed on the National Register of Historic Places. These mine sites include numerous related features such as arrastras (burro-drawn stone ore-grinding site appliances), ore cart run-outs, dry laid and mud masonry stores and housing structures, and carved stone stairways that also require repair and restoration.

ORPI's highest priority challenges consist of developing project proposals to obtain funding for emergency stabilization work at sites including Dos Lomitas Ranch, Bates Well Ranch, Armenta Ranch, Lost Cabin Mine, and Victoria Mine. Additionally, there is the daunting and large-scale need to identify, document, and record hundreds of prehistoric archeological sites that contain earthen and stone architectural remains. These sites, which qualify as Vanishing Treasures resources, contain prehistoric architectural remains that appear on the landscape mainly as earthen water control features such as repressos, bermed reservoirs, and constructed floodwater farming terraces, although many sites also contain bermed "sleeping circles" and stone corrals among other features.

Prehistoric architectural remains of this nature are ephemeral, subtle, and rapidly disappearing from the landscape, particularly in areas of heavy border-related pedestrian and vehicle traffic. It is possible that many of these sites, which are located along ancient trails, could represent sites from the Malpais complex (pre-Clovis). Connie Gibson, the new Archeologist & Cultural Resources Program Manager at ORPI plans to seek funding to intensively survey and document as many Vanishing Treasures archeological sites as possible.

Consultation: Consultation with the Arizona State Historic Preservation Office (AZ-SHPO) and with affiliated tribes is a normal part of doing business at ORPI; and in every

instance, we consider our relationships with consulting parties to be successful and productive.

Safety: Many Vanishing Treasures resources at ORPI are abandoned mines. There are plans to provide safety overhauls of all mines at ORPI that will include securing each mine's shafts, adits, prospect holes, and related features to ensure visitor and employee safety, while at the same time providing multiple-use safe havens for wildlife and threatened and endangered species.

VANISHING TREASURES STAFF

Connie Thompson Gibson, Archeologist & Cultural Resource Program Manager
FY 2005 Position

Connie Thompson Gibson is a registered Professional Archeologist and lithics technologies specialist from Texas, with 15 years' experience in all aspects of cultural resources management. Connie accepted the position at Organ Pipe in October, 2008 and is already furiously busy and immersed in the archeology and history of the Sonoran Desert. She comes to the park with 15 years of field and laboratory analysis experience in Texas; New Mexico; Louisiana; Montana; Belize, Central America; and Chihuahua, Mexico. Her specialties include southwestern archeology and prehistoric lithics technologies including both flaked and ground stone. She has experience as a principal investigator and as a project archeologist in excavation, testing, monitoring, site recording, and National Register site eligibility evaluations. She has conducted prehistoric and historic artifact classification and analyses and has authored professional cultural resource management reports.

Connie received awards from the Bureau of Land Management for her Section 106 compliance work and for her fieldwork related to a large-acreage land exchange. She has recorded, documented, and mapped many new archeological sites throughout the Southwest and the Northern Plains.

Connie has special expertise in site use and National Register eligibility evaluations and is skilled as principal investigator and project archeologist primarily with Class III and Class II large-acreage surveying and testing projects. She is a specialist in lithics technology and National Historic Preservation Act Section 106 compliance.

VANISHING TREASURES PROJECT FUNDING

Organ Pipe Cactus National Monument did not receive project funding this year.

The US/Mexico border cuts an arrow straight swath though the desert, Organ Pipe Cactus National Monument
Photo: Joe Tuomey

Tonto National Monument (TONT)

VANISHING TREASURES ACCOMPLISHMENTS AND CHALLENGES

VT Challenges and Successes: Our greatest challenge has be trying to conduct ruins preservation work among numerous bee hives without getting stung.

Consultation: Tonto staff had a highly successful meeting with the Arizona State Historic Preservation Office (AZSHPO) staff in FY 2008 regarding cultural resources projects requiring Section 106 compliance.

Safety: The ruins preservation projects at Tonto required several planning sessions to accomplish each project safely. For example, a fall-protection specialist and safety officer participated in the planning and design of one project. Overall, the project was a success and no safety incidents occurred.

VANISHING TREASURES STAFF

Duane C. Hubbard, Chief, Resource Management
FY 1998 Position

This position was originally filled as an Exhibit Specialist but has been converted to a Integrated Resource Manager.

Accomplishments: During FY 2008, Duane supervised a variety of cultural resource projects, including preservation projects at back country archeological sites, and continued documentation, preservation and research at five of the primary cliff dwellings in the Monument. Success in acquiring project funding for FY 2008 covered the cost of three additional cultural resources staff members: Matt Guebard, Archeologist; Cinda Ewing, Student Temporary Employee Program (STEP) Maintenance Worker; and Chris Duran, STEP Archeological Technician. This group completed projects related to back country site preservation, implementation of integrated pest management activities in the primary cliff dwellings, and completion of the final preservation work for the park's primary attraction the Lower Cliff Dwelling. Duane continued to establish relationships with numerous affiliated tribes and he managed the park's archeological research, curation, consultation, and compliance.

The original exhibit specialist position was never funded at the full performance level so the park allocated additional base money to fully fund a GS-11 Exhibit Specialist. In

Cultural resources crew performing preservation work at the Lower Cliff Dwelling. Photo: Cinda Ewing

FY 2004 the position was changed to an archeologist (GS-0193-11) with the original VT allocation funding less than ¾ of that position. The position has remained in the 0193 series since FY 2004.

Duane is skilled in conducting condition assessments, architectural documentation, stabilization histories, compliance, and hands-on ruins preservation.

Training: Duane attended contracting officer's representative training in FY 2008.

VANISHING TREASURES PROJECT FUNDING

Project Name: Implement Preservation Treatments at the Upper and Lower Cliff Dwellings (Phase II)

Project Summary: Tonto National Monument requested funding for a treatment project focused on the Lower Cliff Dwelling, Lower Cliff Dwelling Annex, and 24 rooms inside the dripline at the Upper Cliff Dwelling. Phase II of this project (FY 2008) implemented preservation actions including equalizing differential fill loads, improving on-site drainage, replacing eroded mortar through capping and repointing, and mitigating animal disturbance.

Project Budget: $ 109,000
Personnel:	$29,430
Vehicles:	$0
Travel/Training:	$2,180
Supplies/Materials:	$6,540
Equipment:	$0
Services/Contracts:	$70,394
Other:	$456

View of the Upper Cliff Dwelling, Tonto National Monument.
Photo: Rex Lavoie (2009)

Project Accomplishments: Preservation treatment was performed at the Lower Cliff Dwelling which raised this site's condition from "fair" to "good." Preservation crews completed all of the project objectives at the Lower Cliff Dwelling:

(1) preserving prehistoric walls by injecting unamended mortar into areas of insect/animal damage and visitor disturbance;

(2) preserving National Park Service features (stairs, benches, doorways) within the dwelling using stucco and stucco/soil mixtures;

(3) replacing National Park Service gates in Room 15 and 16 to mitigate damage to surrounding original fabric; and

(4) removing ineffective mortar and repointing the retaining wall outside of Lower Cliff Dwelling.

The condition of the Upper Cliff Dwelling, and the large amount of pre-documentation required there, resulted in only minor preservation work being done at this site. Instead, the remaining project funds were used for a contract with Western Mapping for intensive site mapping and surveying. With the completion of this contract, park staff will have all of the documentation required to complete the preservation work on the Upper Cliff Dwelling. This documentation will include architectural sheets with 2D digital and hardcopy images of color-corrected mosaics draped and rectified onto high-resolution 3D models.

Once these final mapping products for the Upper Cliff Dwelling are obtained, the scope of work for the Upper Cliff Dwelling can be finished and staff can commence work on the preservation treatments. This detailed documentation will allow future measurements and characterizations for documentation and stabilization histories to be superimposed on the images. Treatments on the Upper Cliff Dwelling will complete the park's final comprehensive ruins preservation project.

Tumacacori National Historical Park (TUMA)

VANISHING TREASURES ACCOMPLISHMENTS AND CHALLENGES

VT Challenges and Successes:

Consultation: The Vanishing Treasures team at Tumacacori National Historical Park recognizes the need for including the state historic preservation office (SHPO) in the treatment intervention process as early as possible to ensure timely starts to projects. It is a requirement that, when working on other agencies resources, compliance be initiated and approved before beginning the project.

Safety: We have secured for our VT crew training on the proper erection of scaffolding and use of personal protective equip-

The unfinished bell tower of the Mission San José de Tumacácori.
Photo: Randall Skeirik

ment (PPE) while on scaffolding. We have also involved VT subject matter disciplines to provide technical assistance prior to beginning a project. We have utilized the VT structural engineer twice in FY 2008.

VANISHING TREASURES STAFF

Ramon Madril, Masonry Worker
FY 1998 Position

Ray continues to be part of the park's VT team, where he is a highly motivated and proactive preservation mason. Ray has assisted in preservation activities at the park's three units: San Jose de Tumacacori, San Cayetano de Calabazas, and Los Santos Angeles de Guevavi.

Outside the park, Ray was instrumental in rebuilding a fallen wall at the 1880s Fairbank Mercantile in southeast Arizona, where over 4,000 adobe bricks were used to rebuild the west wall of the building. Ray also assisted in the preservation of the historic adobe ranger station in Magdalena, New Mexico, where he replaced beams and other deteriorated structural components of the building, and at the Charleston Mill site (ca. 1860), where he assisted in the stabilization and preservation of the extant adobe walls of this mill located on the banks of the San Pedro River. In this project, over 30 standing adobe walls were stabilized with unamended earth and wall caps, and basal erosion issues were also addressed.

Toward the end of FY 2008, Ray was involved with the rehabilitation of the historic Civilian Conservation Corps (CCC) bridges located at Sabino Canyon in Tucson, Arizona, which were damaged by flooding in 2006.

Ray is a journeyman mason who possesses skills in all facets of historic preservation including earthen architecture, stone, wood, and historic earthen and lime plasters. Ray also assists in conducting workshops to train employees of other state and federal agencies on proper preservation methodologies.

David Yubeta, Exhibits Specialist
FY 1998 Position

David continues to serve as the project manager for park preservation activities at the park's three units.

Beyond the park, he has worked on the Fairbank Mercantile building, the Charleston Mill site, the Magdalena Ranger Station, Fort Lowell Camp, the Terranate Presidio Site, and the historic CCC bridges at Sabino Canyon, all located throughout southeast Arizona. He assisted the Arizona State Historic Preservation Office (AZSHPO) by pro-

Ray Madril and Bobby Jimenez repointing the Camino Loma Alta Lime Kiln at Saguaro National Park.
Photo: Courtesy Tumacacori National Historical Park

viding adobe making training at Tumacacori NHP for the State Historic Preservation Conference. David also continues to provide assistance to Mexican counterparts by arranging venues and preservation training in municipalities in the US and Mexico. Being blessed with a highly motivated and skilled preservation crew, David finds his challenges are minimal.

In addition to his skills in the field of historic preservation and adobe, David has considerable experience in providing historic preservation-related training.

Jeremy Moss, Archeologist, Resource Manager
FY 2000 Position

Jeremy conducted detailed documentation and condition assessments of all the historic structures in the park and analyzed lime plasters to locate original limestone sources. He developed a preservation database and wrote a preservation history of the Mission, is currently completing the 2004-2006 testing report, and is analyzing historic artifacts in the Tumacacori collection. Additionally, Jeremy completed Native American Grave Protection and Repatriation Act (NAGPRA) consultation with the park's affiliated tribes.

Jeremy can assist with project management, condition assessment and documentation,

archeology survey and testing, compliance, and artifact analysis. He is skilled in the areas of archeology, cultural resource management, historic preservation documentation and treatment, natural resource management, and collections management.

Training: Jeremy both attended and helped to organize the TICRAT (Taller Internacional De Conservación Y Restauración De Arquitectura De Tierra *or International Workshop For The Conservation And Restoration Of Earthen Architecture*) Conference and workshops.

VANISHING TREASURES PROJECT FUNDING

Tumacacori National Historical Site did not receive project funding this year.

Vanishing Treasures

California/Nevada

Keys Ranch, Joshua Tree National Park

Photo: Randall Skeirik

◇ Death Valley National Park ◇ Joshua Tree National Park ◇ Mojave National Preserve ◇
◇ Manzanar National Historic Site ◇

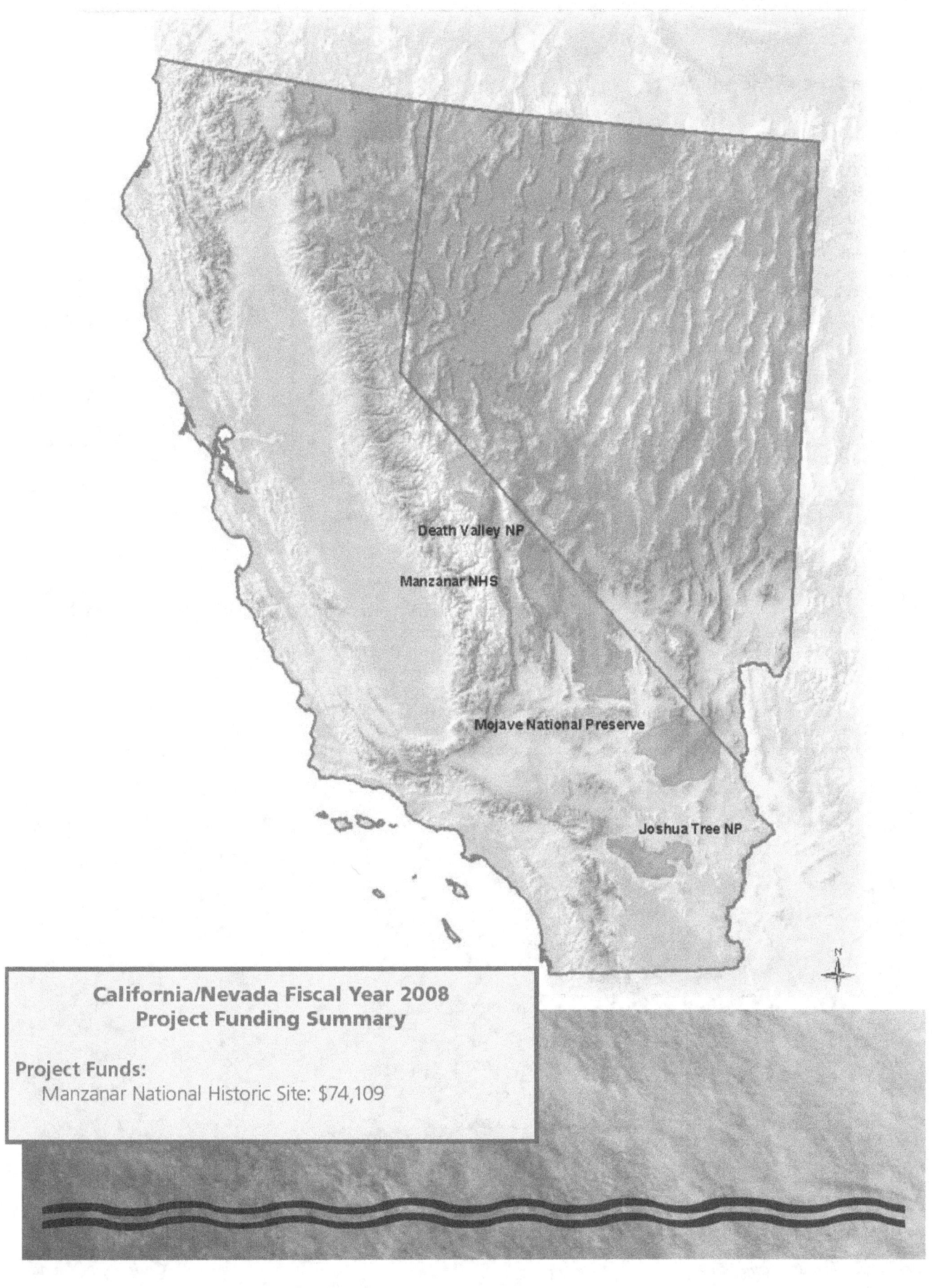

Death Valley NP

Manzanar NHS

Mojave National Preserve

Joshua Tree NP

N

**California/Nevada Fiscal Year 2008
Project Funding Summary**

Project Funds:
Manzanar National Historic Site: $74,109

Joshua Tree National Park (JOTR)

VANISHING TREASURES ACCOMPLISHMENTS AND CHALLENGES

VT Challenges and Successes: The park's highest priority has been to establish baseline documentation of historic structures that are highly susceptible to vandalism, high winds, erosion, and UV degradation. Sites such as Key's Ranch and Wall Street Mill are some of the most visited areas of Joshua Tree and visitors certainly appreciate the stories these sites tell. However, it is a considerable challenge to keep these structures standing as many utilize recycled materials, were built without a formal building plan, and did not use standard construction techniques.

Consultation: Unfortunately, many of our affiliated tribes lack the infrastructure to respond regularly to tribal consultation. Tribes that do respond have been supportive of our efforts to preserve the physical remnants of the mining and ranching era in the park. Although all of our VT resources are from the historic period, many are located atop, or adjacent to prehistoric sites, necessitating an additional level of consideration in compliance issues.

Safety: Joshua Tree's VT Resources, made up entirely of historic-era structures, are frequented by visitors but are often far

Monzogranite monoliths and joshua trees are characteristic of the northwest section of the park, Joshua Tree National Park.
Photo: Randall Skeirik

enough out in the backcountry to preclude full-time employee supervision. Historic mine adits and prospects are presently being "safed" by filling the shafts with polyurethane foam and installing bat gates that will protect both our visitors and our cultural resources staff as they focus on documenting and stabilizing structures at these sites.

VANISHING TREASURES STAFF

Joshua Tree National Park has not received a base increase to fund a Vanishing Treasures position.

VANISHING TREASURES PROJECT FUNDING

Joshua Tree National Park did not receive project funding this year.

The remains of the main house at Ryan Ranch, Joshua Tree National Park.
Photo: Randall Skeirik

Manzanar National Historic Site (MANZ)

VANISHING TREASURES STAFF

Manzanar National Historic Site has not received a base increase to fund a Vanishing Treasures position.

VANISHING TREASURES PROJECT FUNDING

Project Name: Excavate, Document, and Stabilize Features in Accordance with CLR Recommendations

Project Summary: In FY 2008, the largest and most elaborate garden at Manzanar National Historic Site, Merritt Park, was excavated, documented, and stabilized. Constructed as a Japanese-style "stroll garden" by Japanese Americans interned at Manzanar during World War II, Merritt Park became a sanctuary of beauty and nature within the confines of the internment camp. Numerous historic photographs reflect the importance of this community park to the internees. It symbolized their hope for the future as well as their dedication to the well-being of their community. Internees and camp staff alike came here to enjoy solitude as well as companionship. Prior to this project, it was not known how much of the park had survived because the area was buried by sediment and overgrown with vegetation.

Park Archeologist Jeff Burton directed the investigation and stabilization with the assistance of over 100 volunteers and park staff from both Manzanar and Death Valley National Park. Volunteers came from across the country and from as far away as Japan, representing diverse age groups and ethnic backgrounds. Local and regional high school students worked alongside the 91-year-old son of the landscape architect who designed the park.

Project Budget: $74,109

Personnel:	$38,097
Vehicles:	$0
Travel/Training:	$15,220
Supplies/Materials:	$20,792
Equipment:	$0
Services/Contracts:	$0
Other:	$0

Project Accomplishments: Volunteers and park staff worked together to remove vegetation and sediments in the Merritt Park area. Work included the removal of 32 tamarisk trees, 11 locust trees, and one willow tree, as well as much brush and dead wood. Both hand tools (shovels and trowels) and a backhoe were used to excavate over 600 cubic yards of sediments.

Under the sediments, Merritt Park was found to be surprisingly intact, suggesting that the park remained undisturbed when

Merritt Park Garden after restoration, Manzanar National Historic Site.
Photo: Courtesy Manzanar National Historic Site

the Manzanar Relocation Center was abandoned. Two or three major flooding events had deposited sands, gravels, and a lesser amount of silts over the park as flood debris. Some of the artifacts that were found within the fill of the park's ponds were apparently washed in from the hospital dump, located a short distance upslope. Others, such as a lipstick tube, a comb, marbles, and toy tea cups, were likely lost by internees visiting the park.

Numerous features were uncovered during the work, including landscape boulders, rock walls, stepping stones, posts and post holes, waterfalls, two large ponds, and the remains of a tea house. A concentration of 61 short segments of water pipe found in one of the ponds was probably deposited at abandonment. These pipe segments appear to be the only material that was purposefully dumped at the Merritt Park ponds. This contrasts with other ponds that have been excavated at Manzanar that contained abundant building debris.

Stabilization work at the ponds was guided by historic photographs and by the archeological evidence provided by the feature remains. Stabilization included resetting boulders that had fallen out of place, patching concrete, rebuilding a partially collapsed rock wall, reconstructing two of the original three rangui (wood post) walls, and reattaching the stone "head" of a distinctive turtle rock. To stabilize the tea house foundation, border rocks were reset and a new concrete floor was poured to replace the original concrete floor, which had been cracked and shattered and had several large trees growing through it.

Elaborate Japanese-style bridges are represented by two simple, temporary bridges that were constructed where the more elaborate bridges had been located historically. The new bridges will allow visitors to view the pond more closely without damaging the ponds' fragile banks. Mapping and photography, including overhead views, documented all stages of excavation and stabilization, and a detailed archeological report is in progress.

With its significant volunteer component, the project was a successful example community outreach. Those who participated because of their interest in Japanese American history learned about archeology, and those who came because of their interest in archeology learned about Japanese American history. Not only did the residents take pride in the camp during their internment, the Japanese American community continues to do so today, identifying the restoration of the park as a priority during public hearings for the park's Management Plan. This project has uncovered a significant feature of the camp for the public to see, providing a tangible connection to the lives of the internees..

Vanishing Treasures
Colorado

Archeologist Dani Long documenting ledge rooms at Spruce Tree House, Mesa Verde National Park   *Photo: Courtesy Mesa Verde National Park*

◇ Colorado National Monument ◇ Dinosaur National Monument ◇
◇ Mesa Verde National Park ◇

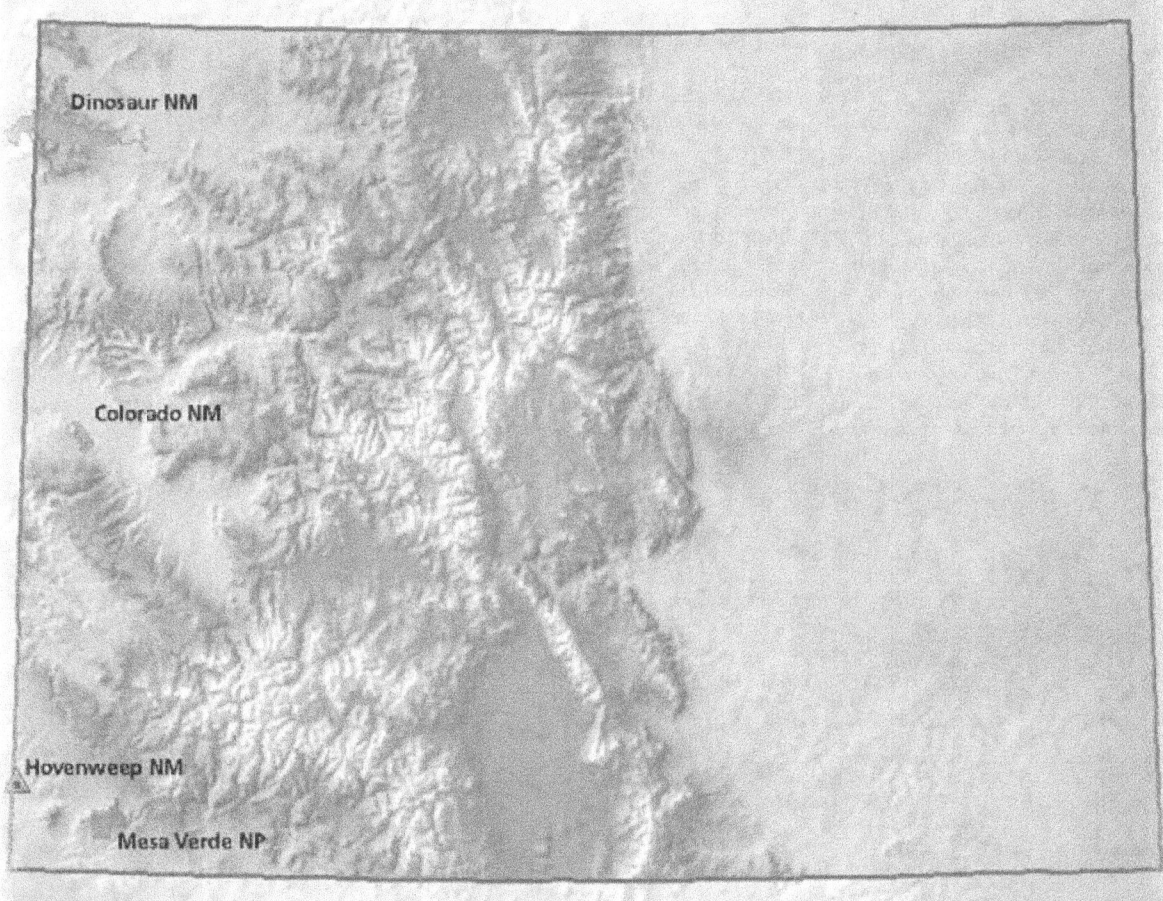

Dinosaur NM

Colorado NM

Hovenweep NM

Mesa Verde NP

**Colorado Fiscal Year 2008
Project Funding Summary**

Project Funds:
    No Colorado parks received project funding.

Mesa Verde National Park (MEVE)

VANISHING TREASURES ACCOMPLISHMENTS AND CHALLENGES

VT Challenges and Successes: Our biggest challenge is our inability to fill vacant Vanishing Treasures positions. Mesa Verde currently has three vacant VT positions: a subject-to-furlough (STF) Exhibit Specialist GS-12 STF (stabilization crew leader), a STF Exhibit Specialist GS-11 (conservator), and a STF Exhibit Specialist GS-9 (stabilization crew member). Funding for the GS-12 position remains within the Division of Research and Resource Management for FY 2008, while the funding for the two lower-graded positions has been absorbed into the overall Park budget. The lapsed salary was used to support a variety of VT-related projects and personnel, including a 120-day detail to move one of our existing Exhibit Specialists into the crew leader position, as well as to shorten the furloughs of four VT positions and to support VT-related training and travel.

A major success of FY 2008 was the use of money from the Centennial Challenge and Cultural Cyclic funding sources to hire two seasonal archeologists to work alongside the four STF members of the stabilization crew. As a result, the crew was able to complete major repairs at Long House, Cliff Palace, and the historic Park Point Fire Lookout Tower and Trail. This was the first time in six years that Mesa Verde was able to hire seasonal positions to help with preservation projects.

Consultation: Mesa Verde National Park has a programmatic agreement with 24 affiliated tribes. This agreement outlines the types of routine assessment, documentation, and preservation methods employed by the Archeological Site Conservation Program. No compliance-related issues were encountered during FY 2008.

Safety: Mesa Verde National Park's VT program had no safety problems or challenges in FY 2008.

VANISHING TREASURES STAFF

Tim Hovezak, Exhibit Specialist
FY 1998 Position

This position was originally filled as a Masonry Worker but has been converted to an Exhibit Specialist.

Tim began the fiscal year by completing a six-year stabilization plan for the Chimney Rock Archeological Area, a site located in the San Juan National Forest. Based on a condition assessment and stabilization project completed by the Mesa Verde stabilization crew in 2006, the final report was presented to the US Forest Service (USFS) in December 2007.

In March and April, Tim was part of a Mesa Verde crew that completed a condition assessment and documentation project on six backcountry alcove sites in Cow Canyon for Glen Canyon NRA, all remarkable for their excellent state of preservation; (See Glen Canyon National Recreation Area for more

Nordenskiold's Ruin No.12 (5MV1321), Mesa Verde National Park.
Photo: Courtesy Mesa Verde National Park

information on this Vanishing Treasures-funded project.) The project involved backcountry camping for nine days and required extensive helicopter support to transport the crew, camping supplies, and equipment to the worksite. Upon returning from this project, Tim compiled an extensive interim report that detailed the work completed in FY 2008, outlining recommended treatments for the six assessed sites.

After the Cow Canyon project, Tim was detailed into the Stabilization Crew Leader position for 120 days, a position that has been vacant since October, 2007. In this capacity, Tim took on the duties of supervising the crew, preparing work plans, prioritizing preservation needs, and managing everyday activities. Under Tim's direction the crew accomplished many preservation projects at Mesa Verde in FY 2008, including work at three of the major frontcountry sites: Cliff Palace, Balcony House, and Long House.

Most of April was consumed by an extensive face lift for Kiva L at Cliff Palace. Sometime after abandonment of the site, the entire south half of this kiva, along with an adjacent multi-story retaining wall, collapsed. The collapsed structures were rebuilt by J.W. Fewkes during the first stabilization effort at the site in the early 20th century. However, Fewkes rebuilt the kiva on loose rubble that subsequently settled, causing displacement and cracking of the wall. Resulting voids in the fill and in the wall had created an appealing environment for rodents, whose burrows contributed to further destabilization of the structure.

At Kiva L, the stabilization effort involved excavation of loose rubble around the entire interior circumference and the placement of new dry stacked masonry to provide a solid foundation for the banquette walls. Work on the walls consisted of repointing and some minor stone replacement. Stabilization of the pilasters and the upper walls was much more extensive, requiring the reconstruction of three collapsed wall sectors,

partial reconstruction of two pilasters, and repointing. The crew also applied a new adobe plaza surface around the south side of the kiva and reset much of the upper masonry on the multistory retaining wall.

At Balcony House, Tim and the crew completed minor repairs to rooms 18, 19, and 20 that involved resetting loose stones that had become dislodged by visitor traffic.

In mid-June, the stabilization crew moved to Long House on Wetherill Mesa to address several critical preservation issues including the addition of new masonry to the front retaining wall and a face-lift to Kiva R similar to that conducted at Cliff Palace earlier in the year. Kiva R is a small masonry kiva located at the far eastern edge of the site where it is exposed to runoff during heavy precipitation events. Direct runoff had dissolved the masonry bonds in the southern recess and along the south wall, resulting

Long House retaining wall prior to stabilization, Mesa Verde National Park.
Photo: Courtesy Mesa Verde National Park

in sagging and partially collapsed masonry. Repairs consisted of repointing and resetting several masonry sections. On the kiva floor, moisture infiltration from water puddles had resulted in hydration damage to the basal coursing and bedrock of the lower walls; which was repaired as necessary. As a final measure, a small quantity of fill was added to protect the floor and provide sufficient slope to channel water away from the walls. The stabilization work at Kiva R was preceded by the field drafting of a complete set of elevation drawings.

Run-off at Long House had resulted in the

erosion of the slope at both the south and front-center of the site, including an area adjacent to the Great Kiva. Most of this erosion had likely occurred immediately after the Pony Fire of 2000 and it was undercutting the modern masonry retaining wall. Photographs taken in 1965, when the site was first stabilized, show a more gradually sloped terrace with more rubble than exists today. In preparation for the project, removal of heavy vegetation exposed several distinct events of wall construction, including some that may be prehistoric. Reinforcement of the wall required the excavation of a footing trench, installation of reinforced concrete footer, and the addition of seven new masonry courses. Finally, the slope below the wall was stabilized with Excelsior matting.

In 2008, some of the responsibility for maintaining historic facilities at Mesa Verde was returned to the Archeological Site Conservation Program. This included the repair and reconstruction of trails, scenic overlooks, and the fire lookout at Park Point. The Park Point facility, distinctive for its modified Pueblo Revival style, is popular for its sweeping view of the park and surrounding landscape. The building itself was constructed as a Civilian Conservation Corps (CCC) project in 1939, with a flagstone apron and nearby masonry overlooks added in later years. The 2008 stabilization work consisted of masonry and other restoration work to the fire lookout, replacing or restoring masonry columns, overall masonry restoration of the overlook platforms, and replacement of part of the flagstone apron around the fire lookout.

The stabilization crew also participated in an experimental project undertaken through a partnership with the historic preservation program at the University of Pennsylvania to test the effectiveness of a new soft cap design for exposed masonry architecture. Similar designs have been successfully applied at locations in the United

Kingdom and Turkey. The methodology consists of placing a series of moisture barriers along wall tops and then capping them with soil and live grass. The experiment was conducted on a short compound partition of wall at Far View House, a large masonry pueblo located on Chapin Mesa. The wall was divided into two parts; one half is being used as a control (a hard cap remains in place), while the vegetative cap was installed in the other half.

Before work began, the wall was first documented using orthorectified photography. Then, half of the hard masonry cement cap was removed and geo-fabric laid on top of the wall core. The geo-fabric was then covered with gravel and soil and was planted with a native bunch grass. Data-loggers were embedded within each capping section to comparatively measure any differences in ambient temperatures and moisture over a one-year period.

Before their winter furlough, Tim and the crew worked on a severely slumping wall at Pipe Shrine House, a Pueblo III mesa top site that is part of the Far View Community. This wall, slumping and leaning more than 30 degrees, was in imminent danger of collapse. The crew rebuilt the wall and part of its foundation before weather brought a halt to the work. They will continue working at Pipe Shrine House in FY 2009.

Finally, Tim and the crew helped with a magnetometer study of a Pueblo I/II village located on Chapin Mesa. The purpose of this study was to locate underground anomalies that may represent early buried pit structures. After identifying six possible buried features, the crew conducted auger testing to help verify the magnetometer results confirming that four of the six features were buried pit structures. These results have helped the park to more accurately interpret this large early Pueblo I/II village.

Tim is skilled in masonry stabilization, site documentation, report writing, testing, excavation, and survey.

Training: Tim attended an historic adobe workshop at Fort Davis in July.

Neill Smith, Masonry Worker
FY 1998 Position

Accomplishments: Neill and the crew accomplished many preservation projects at Mesa Verde in FY 2008 with work accomplished at three of the major frontcountry sites; Cliff Palace, Balcony House, and Long House. Most of April was consumed at Cliff Palace with an extensive face lift for Kiva L. Sometime after abandonment of the site, the entire south half of this kiva, along with an adjacent multi-story retaining wall, collapsed. The collapsed structures were rebuilt by J.W. Fewkes during the first stabilization effort at the site in the early 20th century. However, Fewkes rebuilt the kiva on loose rubble that subsequently settled, causing displacement and cracking of the

STEP employee Stephen Matt and Masonry Worker Neill Smith working on retaining wall at Long House, Mesa Verde National Park.
Photo: Courtesy Mesa Verde National Park

wall. Resulting voids in the fill and in the wall had created an appealing environment for rodents, whose burrows contributed to further destabilization of the structure.

At Kiva L, the stabilization effort involved excavation of loose rubble around the entire interior circumference and the placement of new dry stacked masonry to provide a solid foundation for the banquette walls. Work on the walls consisted of repointing and some minor stone replacement. Stabilization of the pilasters and the upper walls was much more extensive, requiring the reconstruction of three collapsed wall sectors,

partial reconstruction of two pilasters, and repointing. The crew also applied a new adobe plaza surface around the south side of the kiva and reset much of the upper masonry on the multistory retaining wall.

At Balcony House Neill assisted with the completion of minor repairs to rooms 18, 19, and 20 that involved resetting loose stones and that had become dislodged by visitor traffic.

In mid June, the stabilization crew moved to Long House on Wetherill Mesa to address several critical preservation issues including the addition of new masonry to the front retaining wall, and a face-lift to Kiva R similar to that conducted at Cliff Palace earlier in the year. Kiva R is a small masonry kiva located at the far, east edge of the site where it is exposed to runoff during heavy precipitation events. Direct run-off had dissolved the masonry bonds in the southern recess and along the south wall resulting in sagging and partially collapsed masonry. Repairs consisted of repointing and resetting several masonry sections. On the kiva floor, moisture infiltration from water puddles had resulted in hydration damage to the basal coursing and bedrock of the lower walls which was repaired as necessary. As a final measure, a small quantity of fill was added to protect the floor and provide sufficient slope to channel water away from the walls. The stabilization work at Kiva R was preceded by the field drafting of a complete set of elevation drawings.

Run-off at Long House had resulted in the erosion of the slope at both the south and front-center of the site, including an area adjacent to the Great Kiva. Most of this erosion had likely occurred immediately after the Pony Fire of 2000 and it was undercutting the modern masonry retaining wall. Photographs taken in 1965, when the site was first stabilized, show a more gradually sloped terrace with more rubble than exists today. In preparation for the project, removal of heavy vegetation exposed several distinct events of wall construction, including some that may be prehistoric. Reinforcement of the wall required the excavation of a footing trench, installation of reinforced concrete footer, and the addition of seven new masonry courses. Finally, the slope below the wall was stabilized with Excelsior matting.

In 2008, some of the responsibility for maintaining historic facilities at Mesa Verde was returned to the Archeological Site Conservation Program. This included the repair and reconstruction of trails, scenic overlooks, and the fire lookout at Park Point. The Park Point facility, distinctive for its modified Pueblo Revival style, is popular for its sweeping view of the park and surrounding landscape. The building itself was constructed as a Civilian Conservation Corps (CCC) project in 1939, with a flagstone apron and nearby masonry overlooks added in later years. The 2008 stabilization work consisted of masonry and other restoration work to the fire lookout, replacing or restoring masonry columns, overall masonry restoration of the overlook platforms, and replacement of part of the flagstone apron around the fire lookout.

Neill also participated in an experimental project undertaken through a partnership with the historic preservation program at the University of Pennsylvania to test the effectiveness of a new soft cap design for exposed masonry architecture. Similar designs have been successfully applied at locations in the United Kingdom and Turkey. The methodology consists of placing a series of moisture barriers along wall tops and then capping them with soil and live grass. The experiment was conducted on a short compound partition of wall at Far View House, a large masonry pueblo located on Chapin Mesa. The wall was divided into two parts, one half is being used as a control (a hard cap remains in place), while the vegetative cap was installed in the other half.

Before work began, the wall was first documented using orthorectified photography. Then, half of the hard masonry cement cap was removed and geo-fabric laid on top of the wall core. The geo-fabric was then covered with gravel and soil and was planted with a native bunch grass. Data-loggers were embedded within each capping section to comparatively measure any differences in ambient temperatures and moisture over a one-year period.

Before their winter furlough, Neill worked on a severely slumping wall at Pipe Shrine House, a Pueblo III mesa top site that is part of the Far View Community. This wall, slumping and leaning more than 30 degrees, was in imminent danger of collapse. The wall and part of its foundation was rebuilt before weather brought a halt to the work. Neill will continue working at Pipe Shrine House in FY 2009.

Finally, Neill helped with a magnetometer study of a Pueblo I/II village located on Chapin Mesa. The purpose of this study was to locate underground anomalies that may represent early buried pit structures. After identifying six possible buried features, the crew conducted auger testing to help verify the magnetometer results confirming that four of the six features were buried pit structures. These results have helped the park to more accurately interpret this large early Pueblo I/II village.

Neill is skilled in masonry work, repointing, and ruin stabilization.

Training: Neill attended an historic adobe workshop at Fort Davis in July.

Kay Barnett, Exhibit Specialist
FY 2004 Position

Accomplishments: Kay began her season leading a condition assessment and documentation project on six backcountry alcove sites in Cow Canyon for Glen Canyon National Recreation Area. This project involved backcountry camping for 9 days and required extensive helicopter support to transport the crew, camping supplies, and equipment.

Upon her return to Mesa Verde, Kay completed the final field season of the architectural documentation project at Spruce Tree House, a large site that contains 131 rooms, 62 open areas, 31 miscellaneous structures, and nine kivas. This entailed completing the documentation of 35 rooms within the main alcove and nine rooms located on adjacent ledges to the north. Although the ledge rooms had already been recorded and were considered to be associated with the larger portion of Spruce Tree House, previous documentation was very sparse. Completion of this documentation has now provided us with comprehensive documentation of Spruce Tree House.

Kay spent the remainder of the year on the onerous task of data checking more than four years of field work from the Spruce Tree House project. This required cross-checking each electronic record with its corresponding paper record and ensuring that all the maps were complete, accurate, and digitized into AutoCAD. In the coming years we hope to secure funding to complete a comprehensive final report that will highlight the chronological history, construction sequence, and social organization of Spruce Tree House.

Kay is skilled in site documentation, testing, excavation, survey, and stabilization.

VANISHING TREASURES PROJECT FUNDING

Mesa Verde National Park did not receive project funding this year.

Archeologists Joel Gamache and Neal Morris documenting ledge rooms at Spruce Tree House, Mesa Verde National Park. Photo: Courtesy Mesa Verde National Park

Vanishing Treasures

New Mexico

The 18th century church with the Sangre de Cristo Mountains in the distance, Pecos National Historical Park.   *Photo: Angelyn Bass Rivera*

◇ Aztec Ruins National Monument ◇ Bandelier National Monument ◇
◇ Chaco Culture National Historical Park ◇ El Malpais National Monument ◇
◇ El Morro National Monument ◇ Fort Union National Monument ◇
◇ Gila Cliff Dwellings National Monument ◇ Pecos National Historical Park ◇
◇ Salinas Pueblo Missions National Monument ◇

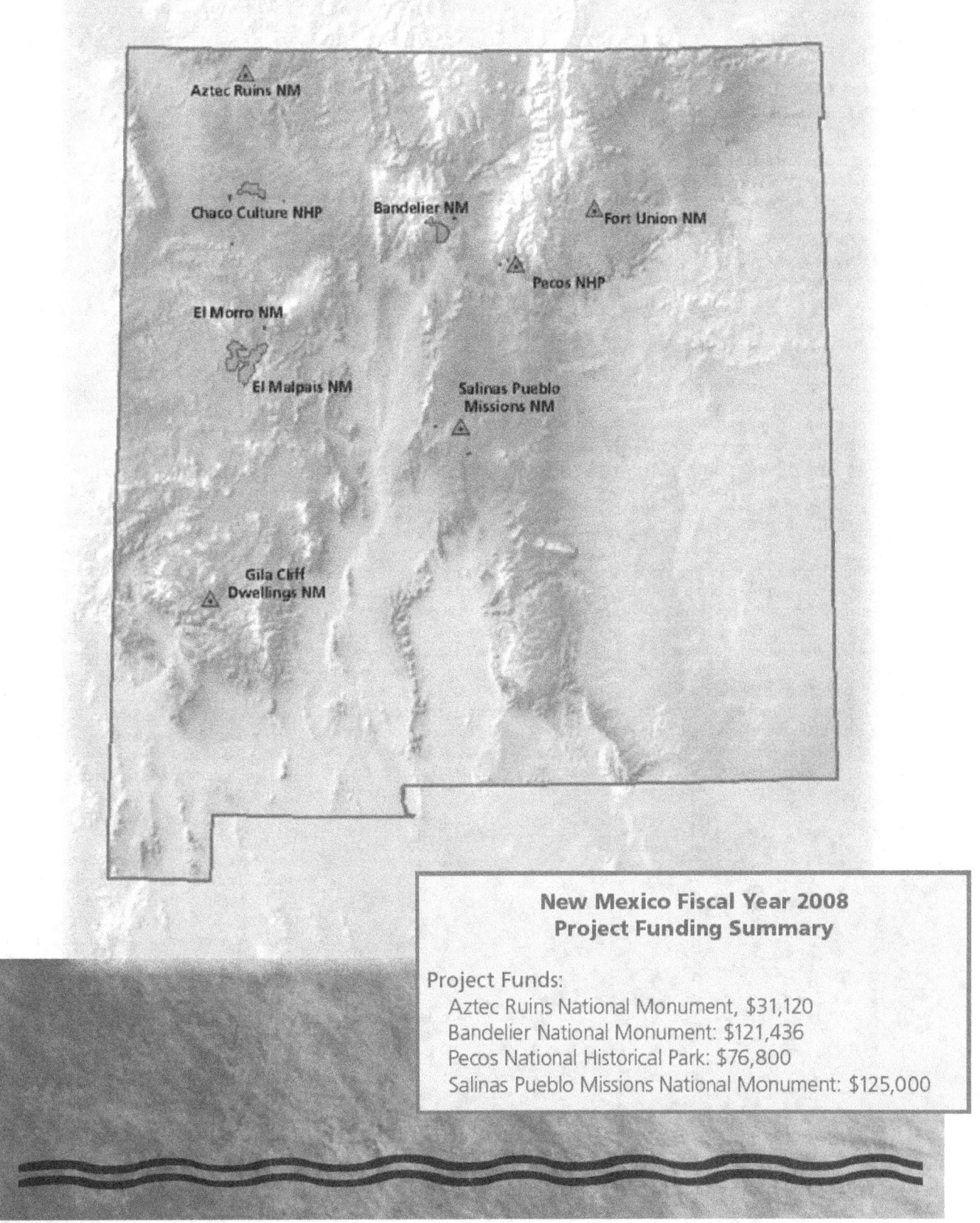

Aztec Ruins NM

Chaco Culture NHP   Bandelier NM   Fort Union NM

Pecos NHP

El Morro NM

El Malpais NM   Salinas Pueblo
Missions NM

Gila Cliff
Dwellings NM

**New Mexico Fiscal Year 2008
Project Funding Summary**

Project Funds:
  Aztec Ruins National Monument, $31,120
  Bandelier National Monument: $121,436
  Pecos National Historical Park: $76,800
  Salinas Pueblo Missions National Monument: $125,000

Aztec Ruins National Monument (AZRU)

VANISHING TREASURES ACCOMPLISHMENTS AND CHALLENGES

VT Challenges and Successes: Our biggest challenge has been the continuing effort to transition from a reactive preservation program aimed at crisis management to a program of preventive maintenance and cyclical preservation treatments. We have achieved a good measure of success in this direction.

Specific preservation challenges during FY 2008 included the removal of old, inappropriate protective roofs from some of the rooms in the pueblo and the design and installation of replacement roofs that will protect intact prehistoric roofs below without adversely impacting other prehistoric fabric in the pueblo. This year, several protective roofs were replaced and one, at West Ruin, was accomplished with VT project funding. (See Vanishing Treasures Project Funding below.)

Consultation: The majority of our historic preservation consultation was accomplished through our annual written report to our affiliated tribes. In addition, project-specific consultation was initiated on modifications to the West Ruin Backfilling Program that includes fill reduction in areas where differential fill cannot be equalized through backfilling. Both the tribes and the New Mexico State Historic Preservation Office (NMSHPO) were generally supportive, but concerns were expressed about the excava-

tion of undisturbed archeological deposits and the removal of artifacts from the site. Consultation on this project and on other routine preservation work continues.

The park is also in the process of preparing a General Management Plan that will provide a standardized platform for further consultation with tribes, NMSHPO, and the public.

Safety: Development of the AZRU Safety Program is ongoing with continued emphasis on Job Safety Analyses (JSAs) and Job Hazard Assessments (JHAs). By involving the preservation crew in the creation of JSAs and JHAs we have established a culture of safety that includes regular tailgate safety sessions with the preservation crew and other cultural resource personnel.

VANISHING TREASURES STAFF

Jeffery T.. Wharton, Exhibit Specialist FY 1998 Position

This position was originally filled as a Masonry Worker but has been converted to an Exhibit Specialist

Jeffery has an extensive background in the archeology of the Colorado Plateau, particularly of the San Juan Basin, along with experience in dealing with a range of cultural resource management concerns. His experience in archeology includes project planning and the development of survey strategies, preparation of data recovery plans, cost estimates and budgets for both small-scale and large block survey and excavation projects, management and execution of cultural resource inventories, coordination and implementation of archeology excavation and testing programs, archeology compliance monitoring, cultural resource recor-

dation and evaluation, synthesis of survey and excavation data, report preparation and editing, geographical information system (GIS) data analysis, computer graphics production, and data/laboratory analysis. His graphics experience includes the mapping and illustration of archeological sites and features, as well as photo-documentation utilizing archeological photographic methods.

In addition, Jeffery has provided environmental monitoring for the Visitor Center curation room and museum, making recommendations for corrective actions when needed. He also conducts environmental monitoring of the ruins including monitoring cracks, recording the temperature and relative humidity inside the intact, protected parts of the ruins, and monitoring the water table in the vicinity of the main ruins group. Information from these activities provides valuable information for the development of, and revision to, our preservation plans. Jeffery also coordinates with the preservation crew and archeologists on numerous preservation, stabilization, and documentation tasks related to the preservation of the pueblo.

His other accomplishments include the archeological survey of the expanded monument boundaries (320 acres) at Aztec Ruins. Ancestral Puebloan sites and other prehistoric and historic properties, including over 50 structural site and cultural landscape features, were documented in this survey. Condition assessments of all of the new sites along with GIS analysis of survey data were part of the overall project. Jeffery also conducted archeological monitoring of various park management projects and served as the cultural resource specialist-participant on the AZRU Vegetation Management Planning Team.

East Ruin preservation projects included involvement in the replacement of protective roofs and gates, responsibility for documenting archeological monitoring results, preparation of sections of the scope of work for the East Ruin stabilization, backfilling, preservation projects, and revisions to the cultural resources section of the AZRU General Management Plan.

At the West Ruin Jeffery worked on backfill adjustments to eliminate soil contact with prehistoric wood door lintels that resulted from rodent damage and on backfill adjustments to reduce impacts caused by differential fill levels. Backfill adjustments also required the installation of drains to help control ground moisture in the ruin.

West Ruin in the snow, Aztec Ruins National Monument.
Photo: Gary Brown

Finally, Jeffery conducted damage assessments of several looted outlying prehistoric structural sites within the expanded monument boundary, providing documentation of the archeological damage, calculating the cost of restoration and repair, and coordinating backfilling in accordance with the Archeological Resources Protection Act (ARPA).

Jeffery's accomplishments include ongoing design and oversight of construction and installation of protective roofs and gates for East and West Ruins, responsibility for the routine environmental monitoring of the Visitor Center and West Ruin, and the installation and monitoring of crack monitors throughout the site.

He is skilled in archeological survey and excavation; cultural resource management; and the design, planning, and construction of protective roofs and protective gates for archeological sites.

Training: Intermountain Region National Environmental Policy Act (NEPA)/Section 106 Workshop, Introduction to GIS metadata creation, editing, & production, Introduction to ASMIS, and Introduction to PEPC (Planning, Environment, and Public Comment).

Gary Brown, Supervisory Archeologist FY 2001 Position

During FY 2008, Gary supervised a sizeable staff that included a number of seasonal hires who augmented existing park personnel. Activities that he supervised ranged from preservation and archeology to curation projects. As Chief of Cultural Resources, he provided oversight for structure and site condition assessments, backfilling and fill adjustments, protective roof maintenance and repair, cultural resource inventory, list of classified structures (LCS) structure documentation, ruins stabilization and minor fabric replacements, and museum collections management. Gary organized and hosted an on-site Vanishing Treasures workshop that focused on backfilling and protective roofing. He also participated in ongoing hydrology monitoring through a cooperative ecosystem study unit (CESU) partnership and in the Middle San Juan Chacoan Outlier research partnership funded by a National Science Foundation (NSF) grant. He participated in the Intermountain Region Resource Stewardship Conference, the Pecos Conference, and the

Aztec Ruins preservation crew stabilizing an ancient kiva, Aztec Ruins National Monument.
Photo: Jeff Heywood

annual meeting of the Society for American Archeology.

Gary is skilled in archeological field techniques, ruins preservation, compliance, artifact analysis, writing and technical illustration, statistical analysis, and project management. He has special knowledge in the areas of backfilling, site conservation, ruins preservation, architectural documentation, and archeological dating.

Ernest Harrison, Masonry Worker FY 1998 Position, Converted to Term, Subject-to-Furlough in FY 2001

This position was held by Carl Jim, who worked on masonry stabilization work during FY 2008 but left the position part way through the year. After his departure, the position was filled by Ernest Harrison.

Ernest, who was already working as a member of the AZRU preservation crew, was being funded through various project fund sources before moving into this position and assuming the role as work leader on the preservation crew. In his new role, he assisted with logistics and implementation of a variety of preservation tasks ranging from routine ruins maintenance to the design and construction of ruins-protecting, free-standing roofs. He set high standards

for masonry fabric treatments and he provided leadership for a crew consisting of masonry workers and unskilled laborers.

Ernest is skilled in masonry ruins stabilization, pre- and post-stabilization documentation, backfilling, protective roofing, preservation, and digital photography. This year he had training in scaffold erection and safety.

VANISHING TREASURES PROJECT FUNDING

Project Name: Replace Three Protective Roofs at West Ruin
PMIS Number: 116535

Project Summary: Rooms 112, 113, and 202 in West Ruin originally had heavy concrete protective roofs that were constructed historically and built into the fabric of the prehistoric walls. They were constructed to protect the original prehistoric roofs that lie underneath. Because these concrete roofs were heavy, they had the potential to negatively impact the prehistoric walls that supported them. The goal for this project was to remove the heavy concrete roofs and replace them with modern, lightweight roofs that would be less intrusive and pose less risk to the historic masonry. These modern roofs will utilize up-to-date materials that are much lighter and more compatible with the appearance of the prehistoric ruin.

Project Budget: $31,120

Personnel:	$27,088
Vehicles:	$0
Travel/Training:	$0
Supplies/Materials:	$4,032
Equipment:	$0
Services/Contracts:	$0
Other:	$0

Project Accomplishments: This project was only partially funded during FY 2008. With the funding available, one of the concrete roofs was demolished and removed without impacts to the original prehistoric roof. It was replaced with a lightweight protective roof of wood and other modern roofing materials that provide substantial protection for the original prehistoric roof below. New roof vents were also installed to allow airflow between the prehistoric roof and the new roof. These vents were constructed to prevent foreign materials, rodents, or other small animals from accessing the air space beneath the protective roof. The remaining two concrete roofs (Rooms 112 and 113) will be replaced in FY 2009

Bandelier National Monument (BAND)

VANISHING TREASURES ACCOMPLISHMENTS AND CHALLENGES

VT Challenges and Successes: The Vanishing Treasures Program at Bandelier National Monument completed work on several projects in FY 2008.

1. VT/Condition Assessment: Tsankawi Cavates
2. Cultural Cyclic: Stabilize Tyuonyi Pueblo
3. Cultural Cyclic: Graffiti Mitigation of Frijoles Canyon Cavates
4. Cultural Cyclic: Stabilize Big Kiva
5. CRPP Base: Conserve Frijoles Canyon Cavates

Although there were a number of challenges to overcome in FY 2008, all of our project goals were met. The success of the Vanishing Treasures Program at Bandelier National Monument can be attributed to the hard work of our crew of term and seasonal archeologists, conservators, masonry workers, archival specialists, along with the contributions of park staff and partners. In addition, Superintendent Brad Traver; Administrative Officer JoAnn Unruh; Contracting Officer Bob Maynard; John Mack and Bob Powell, Chief and Acting Chief of Resources; Mark Mackenzie, Director of Conservation for the Museum of New Mexico Conservation Laboratory; Angelyn Bass Rivera, Conservator at Pecos National Historical Park; and Jeff Brown, Chief of Resources at Pecos National Historical Park all provided a great deal of assistance and support. Masons Marty Davenport (contractor) and Eluterio Varela, Vincent Quintana, and Reynaldo Tafoya of Pecos National Historical Park all contributed to the masonry stabilization project at Big Kiva.

Consultation: The park successfully consulted with the State Historic Preservation Officer and affiliated tribes under Section 106 requirements for work related to the preservation of cultural sites.

Safety: The Vanishing Treasures Program at Bandelier National Monument conducted weekly safety sessions led by different staff members to address issues related to both field projects and office work. These sessions utilized both Job Hazard Analyses (JHAs) developed for projects and outside research. Members of the VT field crew were made aware of the hazards involved in their jobs and took great care to keep themselves and their co-workers safe.

VANISHING TREASURES STAFF

Lauren Meyer, Exhibits Specialist (Conservator)
FY 1999 Position

In May, 2007, Angelyn Bass Rivera stepped down as manager of the Vanishing Treasures Program at Bandelier National Monument. Her position remained vacant until April 2008, when Lauren was hired to fill the vacancy. Lapsed salary was used to support a temporary upgrade for Lauren, who served as acting program manager from October 2007 to February 2008. The remaining funds were used to support other park priorities.

As the Vanishing Treasures program manager at Bandelier, Lauren's responsibilities included the oversight and management of all VT program activities at the park, including the following,

- Emergency Treatment of Frijoles Canyon Cavates (budget $202,000): Exhibit Specialist Shannon Dennison led a crew of archeologists and conservators in the continued treatment of the high-priority cavates in Frijoles Canyon. As a result of this project, several cavates were treated for tuff deterioration, ceiling and wall undercutting, and loss of structural material resulting from improper drainage. In addition to the continued implementation of cavate treatments, Cave Kiva was re-sooted in order to conceal modern graffiti with assistance from Museum of New Mexico conservators Larry Humetewa and Conor McMahon and individuals from the Interpretation Division.

- A workshop, led by professional photographer Moe Nadel, educated crew members on the proper use of cameras and associated equipment, and trained individuals in techniques for photographing the cavates.

- Photography of medium-priority cavates was completed, as was before and after treatment photography on cavates treated in FY 2008.

- $63,000 was obligated through the Desert Southwest Cooperative Ecosystem Study Unit to implement a research project on the anthropogenically disturbed areas of the tuff cliffs in Frijoles Canyon. Bandelier's partner in this project will be New Mexico State University, led by Nancy McMillan, chair of the Department of Geological Studies.

- Funds were obligated, through a contract awarded to 4G/Western Mapping Company, for the mapping of the archeological resources in Frijoles Canyon

- Field crew members took on individual projects related to the cavates in order

Frijoles Canyon. Long House is visible in the lower left, Bandelier National Monument. Photo: Bill Johnson

to enhance their knowledge and understanding of certain features, treatments, and materials.

- Graffiti Mitigation in Frijoles Canyon Cavates (budget $31,439): Through a Cooperative Agreement with the Museum of New Mexico Conservation Department, Conservators Larry Humetewa and Conor McMahon returned to Bandelier in order to assist VT crew members with graffiti mitigation. Approximately 10 cavates were treated in FY 2008.

- Stabilization of Tyuonyi Pueblo (budget $50,000): This stabilization work was led by Exhibit Specialist Shannon Dennison, with assistance provided by Masonry Worker Martin Davenport. The 2008 season consisted of the reassessment of high and medium priority walls, removal of cementitious mortars (where appropriate), and repointing and reconstruction of walls using an acrylic amended earthen mortar. Over the course of the season, a total of 41 wall faces were assessed, treated, and photographed. Funding was also put toward a contract to laser scan standing walls and topographic features of the pueblo.

- Assess and Stabilize Big Kiva (budget $43,500): Following a condition assessment that was conducted in FY 2007, the walls of Big Kiva were stabilized using techniques and materials similar to those that have been used since 2002 to stabilize Tyuonyi Pueblo. Fieldwork was led by Exhibit Specialist Shannon Dennison and assistance was provided by Pecos National Historical Park and Jake Barrow, VT Exhibit Specialist. Treatment of all walls was completed in June 2008. Funds were also put toward a contract to laser scan the interior and exterior walls of Big Kiva.

- Condition Assessment of Tsankawi Cavates (budget $121,436): See VT project narrative below.

Lauren was on maternity leave from September through December, 2008.

Lauren has a background in archaeology and historic preservation and has been employed as an architectural conservator in the NPS since 2001. She has a strong background in documentation, condition assessment, and treatment of archeological sites and architectural features. For the last several years, Lauren has focused on the development and implementation of treatments for stone masonry, earthen mortars, and earth- and lime-based plasters. Lauren is also highly skilled at database development and management as a result of both project work through the Vanishing Treasures Program at Bandelier National Monument, and contracts completed for several Museums and conservation organizations.

Training: Lauren attended Section 106 training through the National Trust for Historic Preservation, as well as basic 40-hour Supervision and NPS safety training.

Shannon Dennison, Exhibits Specialist (Conservator)
FY 1998 Position

This position was vacated in April 2008. In August, 2008, Shannon Dennison was offered and accepted this position. Lapse salary was used for other park priorities.

In FY 2008, Shannon supervised a crew of seven seasonal employees and served as project manager for the Frijoles Canyon cavate conservation project, the Big Kiva masonry stabilization project, and the Tyuonyi Pueblo masonry stabilization project. Shannon also assisted program manager Lauren Meyer in overseeing contracts and administering budgets; and while Lauren was on maternity leave, Shannon took on all responsibilities related to the management of the Vanishing Treasures Program at Bandelier. As a result of Shannon's hard work, all VT projects were completed successfully, within budget, and on schedule.

Shannon has a Master's of Arts in architectural conservation from The University of York (UK) and Bachelor of Arts in anthropology with an emphasis in archaeology and a minor in Native American Studies from The University of Montana. Shannon spent a season at Mesa Verde as an interpreter before attending graduate school and then worked on cultural resource projects throughout the American west. Before coming to Bandelier, Shannon worked for a cultural resource management firm as a historic preservation and archeological project manager. She has a strong interest in the public use and understanding of cultural sites as well as the philosophical and practical issues surrounding the preservation of maintained archeological sites accessible to the visiting public.

VANISHING TREASURES PROJECT FUNDING

Project Name: Condition Assessment of Tsankawi Cavates

PMIS Number: 115760

Project Summary: Location information is known on most of the cavates in the Tsankawi Unit of Bandelier National Monument because much of the area was mapped by Robert Lister in 1939, and again by the Bandelier Archeological Survey between 1986 and 1992. In addition to these maps, studies of select groups of cavates in Tsankawi were undertaken by H. Walcott Toll in 1986 and by Shaun Provencher in 1999 to record architectural information and existing conditions. While these studies provide us with some additional information, it is quite limited.

As part of the Toll study (1986), 116 of the

Masonry Worker Tony Cimmarusti replaces lost mortar in a wall at Long House Pueblo, Bandelier National Monument.
Photo: Rae Miller

more than 300 Tsankawi cavates were assessed and documented. At that time, Toll placed 22% of the cavates that he inspected in a "greater threat" or "major problem" category, and broad treatment recommendations were made. While cavate exteriors were deemed stable, interior conditions in many of them were identified as problematic. Conditions included wear on the tuff and plasters resulting from applied and incised graffiti, deterioration and loss of floor material, masonry collapse, and structural instability as a result of tuff erosion. Although treatment recommendations were made, no treatment program was ever initiated. As Toll's study is now over twenty years old, it is likely that the data no longer reflect the current condition of the cavates.

Following Toll, Shaun Provencher assessed approximately 142 cavates on North Mesa and Tsankawi Mesa in 1999. Provencher recorded that 11% of the cavates assessed were in need of "immediate treatment" and 27% more were flagged as likely to need "future treatment." Erosive conditions similar to those recognized in the Toll study were identified, and treatment recommendations were once again made. These included restriction of access, stabilization of deteriorating tuff (including areas of significant loss and undercutting), plaster conservation (reattachment and edging), and drainage control. Also recommended was the comprehensive and systematic assessment and documentation of the Tsankawi cavates in order to create a body of condition and architectural data. As a result of Provencher's study, 2 cavates were treated for graffiti and plaster conservation measures were tested in one cavate. No additional assessment or treatment programs have been initiated since 1999.

Based on informal visits to Tsankawi by VT staff and results of the limited condition data collected in 1986 and 1999, it was determined that a significant number of cavates are actively deteriorating and will require immediate attention to preserve their remaining archeological value. Conditions that were identified in the earlier documentation remain clearly visible today and include disintegration and abrasion of the tuff walls, cavate ceiling undercutting, detachment/delamination of the multi-layered plasters and washes, and graffiti. The predominant threats to the resource appear to be accelerated erosion caused by water infiltration and unsupervised visitation.

This project focused on a conducting a systematic and detailed recording of existing conditions and an assessment of threats for all the Tsankawi cavates. This information will be used to establish baseline conditions for future monitoring and management and to establish priorities for treatment. Cavate documentation and condition assessment methodology and procedures were developed and used to record over 1,000 cavates in Frijoles Canyon from 2001-2004. These methodologies served as the foundation for this project. The data collected have been added to the customized database that was developed for the cavates of Bandelier National Monument.

Project Budget: $121,436

Personnel:	$1,877
Vehicles:	$0
Travel/Training:	$0
Supplies/Materials:	$0
Equipment:	$0
Services/Contracts:	$119,559
Other:	$0

Project Accomplishments: This project is Phase One of a three-phase conservation project to design and implement a comprehensive conservation plan for the Tsankawi cavates. Specific objectives of Phase One were to complete baseline documentation (architectural descriptions and photographs), conduct systematic and comprehensive condition and significance assessment of Tsankawi cavates, investigate and monitor the environmental causes of their deterioration, and prepare a priority treatment schedule recommending immediate and long-range treatments and monitoring activities for each cavate.

Phase Two will involve hydrogeologic analysis, environmental monitoring, treatment testing, investigative analysis of original materials, and detailed documentation. Phase Three will involve the completion and implementation of a conservation plan for the cavates. The plan will focus on treatments to arrest the causes of deterioration and, to a lesser extent, on repairing existing damage. Utilizing a preventive approach, the plan will allow the resources to retain their integrity by reducing the rate of their deterioration.

The results from all three phases of the project will be used to manage not only the Tsankawi cavates but also hundreds of cavates in adjacent canyons within the park, on the lands of nearby Pueblos and other Federal and State agencies. As an example, Bandelier is currently working with Santa Clara Pueblo to develop a conservation program for the cavates and ruins at Puye.

Phase One of this project was split into three distinct parts:

1. Documentation: Through an agreement facilitated by the Colorado Plateau Cooperative Ecosystem Study Unit (CPCESU), documentation of the Tsankawi cavates was completed by staff of the Office of Contract Archaeology (OCA) of the University of New Mexico (UNM) under the direction of Richard Chapman and Cynthia Herhahn, project Principal Investigators. As part of this agreement, OCA provided services for the following tasks:

a. coordination with park personnel at Bandelier National Monument to develop documentation protocols;

b. participation in field training of the OCA documentation crew by BAND personnel;

c. field checking of existing cavate maps, and selecting a numbering system for the cavates to facilitate documentation and condition assessment;

d. documentation of architectural features and performance of condition assessment for approximately 300 cavates according to established protocols (documentation included digital photography of cavate exteriors, significant architectural features, and unique conditions);

e. recordation of the locations of hand and toe holds, petroglyph panels, and trails that are directly associated with the cavate pueblos;

f. entering collected data into a BAND project database previously developed by park personnel, and;

g. digitization of archival photographs and negatives.

Project deliverables included a brief summary report, updated maps, photo logs, digital image files, database files, CDs of photographs and negatives, and finders guides.

2. Condition assessment: Under the direction of Angelyn Bass Rivera, Exhibits Specialist (PECO), Lauren Meyer, Exhibits Specialist (BAND); and Shannon Dennison, Exhibits Specialist (BAND), seasonal staff at Bandelier National Monument assessed the condition of all extant materials in approximately 333 cavates around Tsankawi Mesa. Fieldwork was completed by Leslie Friedman and Stephen Merkel, seasonal Exhibits Specialists (BAND); Daniel Madryga, Student Temporary Employment Program (STEP) Exhibits Specialist (BAND); and Rebecca Chan and Katy Gallagher, STEP Archeological Technicians (BAND).

The methodologies employed by the field team were based on those developed for the documentation and condition assessment of the Frijoles Canyon Cavates (2000-2007).

Accomplishments included the following:

a. training of three new archeological technicians and three new exhibits specialists in cavate condition assessment methods,

b. assessment of the condition of 333 previously unevaluated cavates on Tsankawi Mesa,

c. production of sketch maps of a previously undocumented cavate group, and

d. production of a detailed sketch map

of an intact and archeologically significant cavate floor.

In addition to the fieldwork, detailed condition data for all assessed cavates were entered into an Access database. These data were used to develop a treatment schedule for the cavates of Tsankawi Mesa.

3. Mapping: Through a contract awarded to 4G/Western Mapping Company of Tucson, Arizona, the cavate pueblos of Tsankawi Mesa, as well as all associated archeological/architectural features, will be mapped

through photogrammetry and GPS. Aerial photographs were taken for the entirety of Tsankawi Mesa in November, 2007, and processing of these photographs and map production are underway. These products will allow Bandelier staff to more accurately locate cavate sites and will serve as a base layer to a Geographic Information System into which all architectural and condition assessment information will be entered. The resulting system will facilitate the monitoring of site conditions and the conservation of the resources around Tsankawi Mesa.

Chaco Culture National Historical Park (CHCU)

VANISHING TREASURES ACCOMPLISHMENTS AND CHALLENGES

VT Challenges and Successes: Our last VT funded project was the backfill of the Pueblo Bonito plazas in FY 2007. While this was last year's project, the tail end of the backfilling spilled over into the beginning of FY 2008 and it represented the last scheduled segment of a Park backfill plan that was outlined for our VT sites nearly 15 years ago. Because of funding shortfalls work on the various sites has taken longer to complete than originally planned, nevertheless, the work itself has been a great success.

Thousands of square feet of wall fabric have been treated, covered by fill, and removed from our cyclic treatment work load. At some of the backfilled sites, the reduction in the amount of wall fabric needing cyclic treatment represents a large percentage of the exposed walls surfaces (eg. Pueblo Alto, BC50, BC 51, BC 59). For others, the proportion of fabric now protected by backfill represents only a small proportion of the exposed walls, but the backfilling solved serious and widespread drainage problems within the site (eg Pueblo Bonito, Chetro Ketl, Pueblo del Arroyo). At every site, drainage systems were either installed or existing drainage systems enhanced. Early experiments with drainage and wood protection, conducted in partnership with the Getty Conservation Institute, were examined, re-evaluated, and modified for various localized situations over the course of the

program.

Having completed this extensive and long-term backfill program, we will be monitoring the sites and fine-tuning the backfilling and drainage systems as needed while turning our primary focus to cyclic maintenance.

One of our goals for the near future is to obtain funding to allow us to consolidate the backfill records and create a final backfill report for the entire project.

For more information about the Chaco backfilling project see "VT Backfilling at Chaco Canyon and Aztec Ruins" in the FY 2007 Vanishing Treasures *Annual Report*.

Consultation: Our last VT funded project was backfill of the plazas at Pueblo Bonito in FY 2007. Decades of visitor traffic and natural erosion from both wind and water had caused the well built drainage systems in the east and west plazas to become the highest points in the plazas. The backfill project corrected this so that all areas of the two plazas would drain to the existing drainage system. Consultation with the tribes posed no problems, as there would be no excavation into prehistoric fill and the project would restore the plazas to the surface conditions existing in the 1950s. We have a good working relationship with the 23 tribes with which we consult as well as with the New Mexico State Historic Preservation Office (SHPO). Presentations of cyclic maintenance proposals for our VT sites are typically the least controversial aspect of our tribal consultations, and have been met with support from the New Mexico SHPO.

Safety: The Chaco preservation division maintains a set of over 20 job safety analyses (JSAs) for our preservation related work. This includes all backfilling related activi-

View from a doorway in the Chetro Ketl Greathous Park.

Photo: Courtesy Chaco Culture National Historica

ties, masonry repair and treatment, drainage setups, removing water collected in basins within sites after storms, use of front-end loaders, dump trucks, conveyor and electric generator setups, scaffolding, climbing skills and equipment, welding, use of mortar mixers and other equipment. The preservation crew reviews these JSAs on a regular basis, especially when beginning a new project. The crew also receives Red Cross first-responder training every year.

While our safety record is not perfect, we have avoided serious injuries while working on VT sites for over seven years. It is a challenge to keep the safety awareness level relatively high, especially during the hottest part of the summer season. Holding a tail-gate meeting every morning before leaving for the field, and reminding all crew members

that they can stop a project if they see an unsafe act or situation has helped maintain a relatively high safety awareness level.

VANISHING TREASURES STAFF

Roger A. Moore, VT Archaeologist
FY 1999 Position

Roger has acquired significant on-the-job training in masonry work and testing of mortar mixes, and has formal training in general preservation techniques, lithic artifact analysis, lithic materials identification and analysis, National Environmental Policy Act and Section 106 of the National Historic Preservation Act compliance, and Archeological Resources Protection Act investigations and incident reporting. Roger is skilled in the design of preservation docu-

mentation, the evaluation of treatment options, mortar mixing and color experimentation, scaffold safety, lithic technology, and working with and supervising multi-ethnic preservation and archeological crews.

He is skilled in Special Emphasis Program Allocation System (SEPAS) proposal writing, preservation program planning, preservation documentation, and database design and monitoring. Roger serves as the park's Archeological Sites Management Information System database coordinator and maintains scaffold use and safety certification as well as Professional Rescuer certification.

Leo Chiquito, Masonry Worker
FY 1999 Position

Leo is a very skilled masonry worker, having worked for many years doing wall facing repointing, stone replacement, wall core rehabilitation, wall basal repair, and wall capping construction and repair.

He is very experienced in mud and cement mortar repair on prehistoric and historic stone structures, backfill operations, and the design and construction of pipe drainage systems associated with backfilling.

Training: Leo's training this year included a formal three-day scaffolding training program, Lay Responder First Aid and CPR training, and the annual NW New Mexico VT workshop.

Earl Johnson, Work Leader
FY 1999 Position

Earl is a master mason with 30 years of experience working on many of the sites in the park as well as on greathouses and Navajo pueblitos. He has been involved in the backfilling program since it started nearly 14 years ago. As a work leader he both takes part in the work and teaches his crew in all aspects of ruins stabilization and backfilling. He has experience in managing multiple preservation crews involved in different levels of ruins treatment at several sites.

In addition to his long history of masonry work, Earl has learned to estimate the personnel time needed to carry out various preservation and backfill activities and assist with estimates of project time and cost for SEPAS project proposals. He speaks both English and Navajo and can supervise employees in both languages.

Training: Earl's training this year included a three-day scaffolding training program, Lay Responder First Aid and CPR training, and he attended the NW New Mexico VT workshop.

e looking southward across Chaco Canyon to South Mesa, Chaco Culture National Historical

l Park

Preservation Crew Leader Earl Johnson repairing capping on a second story wall at Wijiji Greathouse, Chaco Culture National Historical Park.
Photo: Courtesy Chaco Culture National Historical Park

James Yazzie, Masonry Worker
FY 1999 Position

James is a skilled masonry worker, having spent many years doing wall facing repointing and stone replacement, wall core rehabilitation, wall basal repair, and wall capping construction and repair. James is very experienced in mud and cement mortar repair on prehistoric and historic stone structures, backfill operations, and the design and construction of pipe drainage systems associated with backfilling. James has employed his skills on prehistoric greathouses and unit pueblos, proto-historic Navajo pueblitos, and historic Navajo hogans and ornos.

James has played an important role in our drainage system design and backfill program over the last 12 years, operating a small front end loader, setting up the conveyor system, and operating the generator. He has also served as one of our photographers for documenting before and after treatment.

Training: Earl's training this year included a three-day scaffolding training program and Lay Responder First Aid and CPR/AED training, and he attended the NW New Mexico VT workshop.

Garry Joe, Masonry Worker
FY 2002 Position

Garry is a skilled masonry worker, with many years of experience in wall facing re-

pointing and stone replacement, wall core rehabilitation, wall basal repair, and wall capping construction and repair. In addition, Garry maintains a commercial driver's license and can operate a dump truck, front end loader, and Bobcat loader. He is very experienced in mud and cement mortar repair on prehistoric and historic stone structures, backfill operations, and the design

and construction of pipe drainage systems associated with backfilling.

Training: Garry's training included a formal three-day scaffolding training program, Lay Responder First Aid and CPR/AED training, and the annual NW New Mexico VT workshop; and he maintains an LCD license.

Harold Suina, Masonry Worker
FY 2001 Position

Harold is a skilled masonry worker, with many years working on prehistoric wall facing repointing and stone replacement, wall core rehabilitation, wall basal repair, and wall capping construction and repair. Harold has employed his skills on prehistoric greathouses and unit pueblos, proto-historic Navajo pueblitos, and historic Navajo hogans and ornos. Harold is very experienced in mud and cement mortar repair on prehistoric and historic stone structures, backfill operations, design and construction of pipe drainage systems associated with backfilling. In addition he keeps track of and completes most of the documentation forms for backfilling.

Training: Harold's training this year included a three-day scaffolding training program and Lay Responder First Aid and CPR/AED training, and he attended the NW New Mexico VT workshop.

VANISHING TREASURES PROJECT FUNDING

Chaco Culture National Historical Park did not receive project funding this year.

Preservation crew leader Earl Johnson discusses preservation treatments with Cultural Resource division chief Dabney Ford, Chaco Culture National Historical Park.
Photo: Courtesy Chaco Culture National Historical Park

El Malpais National Monument (ELMA)

VANISHING TREASURES ACCOMPLISHMENTS AND CHALLENGES

VT Challenges and Successes: The management of museum collections related to Vanishing Treasures resources and projects is the most significant challenge facing the program at El Malpais National Monument. Each day in the field generates information that is recorded in some fashion. Projects generate linear feet of archives, and condition assessments and inventories often discover objects that are collected to prevent them from being stolen. This presents a challenge because it may become the responsibility of VT staff, especially at parks that do not have curators, to properly care for museum collections. Multiple annual inventories, completion of museum standards checklists, and the National Catalog submittal all require attention, time, funding, and personnel qualified to manage museum collections. El Malpais suggests that the Vanishing Treasures Program evaluate this need and determine if a curator position should be funded to assist parks on a program-wide basis.

Our most successful project of 2008, executed by the VT Program at El Malpais, was the completion of routine preservation maintenance to the Garrett Homestead, a Depression-Era structure located in the Sandstone Bluffs area of the monument. Preservation treatments included repointing eroded mortar joints and resetting loose masonry throughout the one-room structure. Although the homestead is not formally interpreted, it is located alongside one of the main roads within the monument and is often visited. With Mt. Taylor rising over 11,000 feet in the distance, the structure creates a picturesque image for photographers.

Consultation: El Malpais has developed and maintained very good relationships with the New Mexico Historic Preservation Division and Indian tribes in New Mexico and Arizona. In FY 2008, El Malpais consulted these offices regarding a number of projects, but most specifically for fire management undertakings. Vanishing Treasures resources must be inventoried and evaluated for potential effects prior to any fire management activity. Consultation with outside agencies is required, but El Malpais National Monument considers it the best way to make good decisions about the preservation of cultural resources.

Safety: One of the most significant challenges regarding safety at El Malpais is the ruggedness of the lava flows and the sheer size of the monument. Often, staff must hike across miles of jagged basalt in order to conduct a condition assessment or record a resource. Falls, tripping hazards, cuts and bruises or worse are all potential safety issues related to accessing a resource. While in the field, staff must observe weather conditions, because the lava flows can attract hundreds of lightning strikes per storm during the summer monsoons. Numerous rattlesnakes were encountered during fieldwork in the summer of 2008, as were bobcats.

Despite these challenges, the staff of El Malpais has maintained a good safety record.

VANISHING TREASURES STAFF

James W. Kendrick, Archeologist
FY 1999 Position

Jim directed multiple Vanishing Treasures Projects at El Malpais and El Morro National Monuments in FY 2008. At El Malpais National Monument, the highest priority VT project focused on routine preservation maintenance at the Garrett Homestead.

Hundreds of square miles of jagged black lava flows give El Malpais (the Badlands) its name, El Malpais National Monument.
Photo: Randall Skeirik

Efforts at the Depression-Era homestead concentrated on repointing eroded mortar joints and resetting loose or fallen masonry throughout the one-room sandstone structure.

In order to meet an ever-increasing need concerning management of museum collections, Jim worked with the Western Archeological and Conservation Center in Tucson and the Colorado Plateau Cooperative Ecosystem Study Unit (CPCESU) to develop a multi-year agreement with the University of Arizona to assist El Malpais and El Morro with its annual collections responsibilities. He also worked with other partners who are currently conducting projects at El Malpais and El Morro. These partners include the University of Pennsylvania's Historic Preservation Department, Anthropology Departments at Northern Arizona University and Southern Methodist University, the Center for Desert Archaeology, and the University of New Mexico.

Jim also served as Chair of the Intermountain Region's Resource Stewardship Advisory Team (RSAT) in 2008. RSAT was one of the sponsors of the first comprehensive resource stewardship conference in the Intermountain Region in nine years. Both the Vanishing Treasures Program and archeologists from around the region held affinity meetings during the conference.

Jim's skills include field archaeology, project direction, and cultural resource program management. Jim also specializes in program management, archeological project direction (including data recovery and survey), and cultural resource compliance.

Calvin Chimoni, Masonry Worker
FY 2001 Position

In FY 2008, Calvin led the Vanishing Treasures preservation crew at the Garrett Homestead Preservation Maintenance Project. The Garrett Homestead site contains the remnants of a one-room structure constructed of sandstone masonry that dates back to the late 1930s. The homestead is one of El Malpais' most visited VT resources. Preservation treatments included photographic documentation, repointing of eroded mortar joints, and resetting of loose or fallen masonry throughout the entire structure.

Calvin also led the preservation crew at Atsinna Pueblo atop Inscription Rock at El Morro National Monument. The Atsinna Pueblo Preservation Project is an on-going, multi-year project focused on architectural documentation and preservation of the 700-year-old structure. The most significant accomplishment of 2008 was the development of a soil cement appropriate for use at Atsinna. A key characteristic of this new soil cement is its reversibility. Calvin and Masonry Worker Edwin Seowtewa of El Morro National Monument were instrumental in its testing and developing this new formula.

Central to the success of these projects were condition assessments, treatment recommendations, and the prioritization of preservation needs before any "hands-on" work began. Calvin directed these efforts at both Garrett and Atsinna, which ensured that the most threatened architecture received preservation treatments in 2008.

Calvin has exceptional preservation skills, especially with masonry and earthen materials. Calvin also con-

ducts architectural documentation through photography, conducts architectural condition assessments, and determines appropriate preservation treatments. Calvin's specialties include historic preservation, architectural documentation, and archeological survey and documentation.

VANISHING TREASURES PROJECT FUNDING

El Malpais National Monument did not receive project funding this year.

El Morro National Monument (ELMO)

VANISHING TREASURES ACCOMPLISHMENTS AND CHALLENGES

El Morro is co-managed with El Malpais National Monument and its Vanishing Treasures work is combined with that of El Malpais. Like El Malpais, El Morro's highest priority challenge is the management of our museum collections. While archives and museum objects are not technically considered VT resources, the preservation work that the ELMO VT Program conducts creates a significant backlog of uncataloged items (photos, condition assessments, technical reports, architectural sheets, maps, and so forth). Program-wide, there appears to be no clear strategy for the long-term management of these resources. Parks that have curators do not have this problem; but for those parks that do not, the "challenge" to properly care for museum collections becomes a responsibility that often falls on the shoulders of VT staff.

As noted previously in the report from El Malpais, multiple annual inventories, completion of museum standards checklists, and the National Catalog submittal all require attention, time, funding, and personnel qualified to manage museum collections. El Morro recommends that the VT Program evaluate this need and determine if a curator position should be funded to assist parks on a program-wide basis.

Consultation: El Morro National Monument has a very good relationship with the New Mexico Department of Historic Preservation and with Indian tribes in New Mexico and Arizona. In 2008, consultation with the New Mexico Department of Historic Preservation focused on fire management activities at El Morro. Consultation with Indian tribes focused on Native Ameri-

Calvert Ondelacy repointing the Garrett Homestead, El Malpais National Monument.
Photo: Courtesy El Malpais National Monument

Calvin Chimoni resetting loose stones at Atsinna Pueblo, El Morro National Monument. Photo: Courtesy El Morro National Monument

can Graves Protection and Repatriation Act (NAGPRA) issues. In August 2008, El Morro held a very successful meeting at the Western Archeological and Conservation Center (WACC) with numerous tribes in order to begin a cultural affiliation study.

Safety: In FY 2008, the Vanishing Treasures preservation crew had an excellent season with no near misses or injuries reported while conducting work at Atsinna Pueblo (El Morro) and the Garrett Homestead (El Malpais). Daily tailgate discussions were conducted and all routine work required the use of Job Hazard Analyses and the program's safety plan. Potential hazards at El Morro and El Malpais include falling and tripping hazards, improper use of tools, hiking across rugged terrain, seasonal hazards (heat exposure, poisonous and biting insects/snakes, allergens, lightning, etc.), and lifting and repetitive activities. Most importantly, the daily participation and good communication of the crew members promoted a safe working environment for everyone.

VANISHING TREASURES STAFF

Steven M. Baumann, Archeologist
FY 2001 Position

This position was originally filled as a mason but has been converted to an archeologist

Steve directed Vanishing Treasures projects at Atsinna Pueblo (at El Morro) and El Malpais' Garrett Homestead. Work continued on the Atsinna Pueblo Preservation Project in 2008; accomplishments included the repointing of eroded mortar joints on eight walls in seven different rooms, filling deep voids with mortar, resetting fallen masonry, and repairing severely eroded walls (a result of the summer monsoons). Routine preservation maintenance treatments such as repointing mortar joints and resetting loose and fallen masonry were also conducted at the Garrett Homestead.

Steve also worked closely with the fire management program at both El Malpais and El Morro. At El Morro, he ensured the protection of numerous Vanishing Treasures resources during a fuels thinning project atop Inscription Rock. Steve also worked with several El Morro partners, including the University of Pennsylvania's Historic Preservation Department (UPenn) and the Center for Desert Archaeology (CDA). UPenn began working on a cultural landscape report for El Morro and the CDA is continuing its laser scanning project.

Steve's specialties include archeological project direction and information management; he is qualified to act as a Cultural Resource Advisor during fire incidents or fire management activities. Steve has exceptional field archaeology skills and is an expert in the use of the Archeological Sites Management Information System (ASMIS). He has extensive field experience and has worked in numerous national parks in several different regions. Complementing these skills is his ability to develop and manage large cultural resource information systems, his knowledge of geographical information systems (GIS), and his ability to integrate GIS with other information systems. Steve has managed several major Vanishing Treasures projects; and he holds a red card and has acted as a Resource Advisor on prescribed burns at ELMA.

VANISHING TREASURES PROJECT FUNDING

El Morro National Monument did not receive project funding this year.

McCarty's Lava Flow, El Malpais National Monument. Photo: Randall Skeirik

Fort Union National Monument (FOUN)

VANISHING TREASURES ACCOMPLISHMENTS AND CHALLENGES

VT Challenges and Successes: The major challenge facing the Fort Union preservation staff this year was dealing with the elements, including the severe rain, wind, and hail storms that occurred in late June and again in mid-July. These two major events brought driving rains, hail greater than one inch in diameter, and sustained winds of up to 40 miles an hour. In total, major impacts to the earthen shelter coat resulting from these storms exceeded 7,500 square feet. Significant damage was concentrated on the upper fifth of many north-facing walls; damage that tripled the staff's workload and required many hours to reapply up to three coats of earthen plaster. The summer preservation team, consisting of two crews of masons and laborers, applied an additional 122,600 square feet of earthen plaster.

Consultation: Fort Union management staff met with the Wyoming State Historic Preservation Office (SHPO) and Cultural Resource Support Office staff in late August to discuss current and upcoming projects and to provide new SHPO staff with an opportunity to become familiar with the amazing resources found at Fort Union.

Safety: For the third consecutive year, Fort Union had no work related injuries. All members of the preservation staff are on the safety committee and are extremely committed to a safe environment for employees and visitors alike. Job Hazard Analyses (JHAs) are reviewed and updated at the beginning of the season, and are referred to by staff when needed. Biweekly tailgate safety meetings and on-the-spot jobsite safety walk-bys were conducted on a regular basis throughout the summer as well. One member of the preservation team attended a week-long scaffolding training session held in Albuquerque and, upon his return, shared the information learned with his fellow crew members.

VANISHING TREASURES STAFF

Greg Phillipy, Exhibit Specialist (Ruins Preservation)
FY 2002 Position

Greg vacated the Exhibit Specialist position in April, 2008; the resulting lapsed salary was used to hire additional summer preservation staff. Greg's skills and knowledge in historic preservation and in graphic design will be missed. We hope to have this vacancy filled by early in calendar year 2009

Training: Greg attended Facility Management Software System (FMSS) training in February.

Theodore Garcia, Craft Specialist
FY 2005 Position

Ted continued to utilize his great abilities as a work leader in yet another successful preservation season. Despite weather-related setbacks, Ted and his fellow preservation crew members stabilized all of the adobe structures throughout the Monument, securing them for another winter. In addition to overseeing the application of more than 122,000 square feet of earthen plaster, Ted and the crew repaired a partial wall failure within the Hospital Complex. This failure occurred when torrential rains infiltrated a section of wall that had been previously weakened by a pack rat nesting atop a wooden lintel. Approximately 200 adobes had to be made and relaid in this stabilization effort.

VANISHING TREASURES PROJECT FUNDING

Fort Union National Monument did not receive project funding this year.

The Fort Union preservation crew repoints a stone foundation, Fort Union National Monument.
Photo: Courtesy Fort Union National Monument

Pecos National Historical Park
(PECO)

VANISHING TREASURES ACCOMPLISHMENTS AND CHALLENGES

VT Challenges and Successes: Pecos National Historical Park faced two major challenges at two of its Vanishing Treasures resources this year. The first involved the questions of authenticity and integrity of the17th- and 18th-century adobe church and convento complex, which is the park's key interpretive site. The church and convento were built over a major pre-Hispanic pueblo, and the church and convento walls have been extensively restored and maintained for nearly a century but often still encase original building fabric. It is challenging to validate the importance of the restored walls (which have significant interpretive and historic value) and to obtain sufficient funding to maintain both the original and restored fabric.

The second challenge is the preservation and interpretation of the Pigeon's Ranch complex and its surrounding cultural landscape within its modern context. Pigeon's Ranch is located only a few feet from heavily traveled Highway 50, one of two major access routes into Pecos Village. The building's proximity to this highway creates serious preservation problems for this adobe building, including traffic vibration and road maintenance activities (e.g. snowplows piling snow against the building). Ironically, Pigeon's Ranch is relatively inaccessible to visitors because of the extreme safety hazards posed by vehicular traffic.

We are meeting these challenges with slow and steady success. A preservation plan for the church and convento is in preparation, which will help to define the values of the site and may help to validate the importance of the restored walls. Pecos has requested technical assistance from the Vanishing Treasures historical architect in developing this plan in FY 2009. At Pigeon's Ranch, the park is working with the New Mexico Department of Transportation to improve the safety and maintenance practices associated with the road. We are also implementing new interpretive strategies that include developing trails to allow landscape-level viewing of the site from the northern bluff, as well as designing interpretive brochures and signs that will tell the story of Pigeon's Ranch at the new visitor contact station nearby.

Pigeon's Ranch awaiting re-roofing, Pecos National Historical Park.
Photo: Courtesy Pecos National Historical Park

Consultation: Section 106 compliance was completed for stabilization of Pigeon's Ranch with a State Historic Preservation Office (SHPO) concurrence of "no adverse effect" (see project description below).

Safety: Pigeon's Ranch sits within three feet of New Mexico State Highway 50, a busy thoroughfare between Glorieta and Pecos Village. Re-roofing and basal stabilization along the south side of Pigeon's adobe wall required scaffolding to be placed in the westbound lane of the highway. For four days, the westbound lane of traffic was closed to provide safety for the traveling public and for National Park Service personnel working on the project. To close that lane of traffic, a traffic safety plan was drafted by PECO law enforcement and a New Mexico Department of Transportation (NMDOT) Traffic Control/Roadway Work permit was submitted and approved by the NMDOT; a state-approved traffic control firm was contracted to implement the traffic safety plan and provide all equipment and services for the work; and PECO positioned electronic signs to alert both eastbound and westbound drivers of traffic delays following New Mexico State Highway Department guidelines. The work was conducted in full compliance of state laws and was completed successfully without incident.

VANISHING TREASURES STAFF

Pecos National Historical Park has not received funding for any Vanishing Treasures positions.

VANISHING TREASURES PROJECT FUNDING

Project Name: Stabilize Architecture at Pigeon's Ranch/Repair Pigeon's Ranch Structures
PMIS Number: 73055/116377

Project Summary: This project provided for the re-roofing and basal stabilization of the walls of Pigeon's ranch.

Project Budget: $76,800

Personnel:	$48,644
Vehicles:	$6,011
Travel/Training:	$0
Supplies/Materials:	$16,246
Equipment:	$
Services/Contracts:	$4,750
Other:	$7,768

Project Accomplishments: Project accomplishments at Pigeon's Ranch in 2008 included the following:

(1) Re-roofing of the adobe structure with cedar shakes that were determined (through historic photographs) to be appropriate for the period of significance. The existing deteriorated asphalt roll roofing was left in place. Section 106 compliance was completed prior to implementation. Re-roofing was done in cooperation with the historic preservation crew from Bandelier National Monument.

(2) Stabilization of the building foundation and the lower courses of the adobe walls by replacing eroded adobes, repointing, and re-stuccoing with physically compatible earthen materials. The foundation was fully covered with soil as part of the regrading and drainage effort.

(3) Modification of site drainage and localized soil regrading to promote positive flow of surface water runoff away from the walls. Archeology compliance and investigation was completed prior to regrading.

(4) Removal of ineffective gutters on north and south sides of the building to facilitate water transport from the roof and away from the adobe walls.

(5) Written and photographic documentation before, during, and after treatment. A final report and preservation schedule for Pigeon's Ranch is in preparation.

The long-term plan for Pigeon's Ranch is to open the site to limited public visitation on a guided basis. To do this, future site preservation will focus on increasing safety for employees and visitors and preserving the site's integrity and significance

Salinas Pueblo Missions National Monument (SAPU)

VANISHING TREASURES ACCOMPLISHMENTS AND CHALLENGES

VT Challenges and Successes: Salinas experienced a very busy year in FY 2008 with two Vanishing Treasures-funded projects: the Completion of the Documentation of the Abó Mission (PMIS 117133) and the Stabilization of the San Buenaventura Mission Complex (PMIS 37683). The documentation of the Abó Mission consisted of 3D laser scanning of the mission church and a ground-penetrating radar (GPR) survey of the area immediately surrounding the mission complex. The stabilization of San Buenaventura Mission at Gran Quivira ran from March, 2008 to the end of the fiscal year. While a great deal of work was accomplished, considerable sections of the mission remain to be finished, because both

time and funding were exhausted. The park will use other funding to cover the cost of the labor needed to complete stabilization in FY 2009. All of the necessary materials and supplies have already been purchased with the VT project funds. One focus of the project was to employ and mentor seven disadvantaged students from the immediate area to work on this project. Hired through the Student Temporary Employment Program (STEP), the students were mentored in historic preservation techniques and NPS protocols.

Consultation: Both the Abó and San Buenaventura projects were conducted using categorical exclusions, the templates for which had been previously reviewed by the State Historic Preservation Office (SHPO).

Safety: As our projects were executed, we conducted routine safety sessions related to scaffold and materials handling. In addition, we sent five employees to a fall-protection class sponsored by the Facility Management Division at Petroglyph National Monument.

VANISHING TREASURES STAFF

Ramona Lopez, Maintenance Worker (Ruins Preservation)
FY 1998 Position

This position was vacant during part of FY 2008. Because of extended leave taken by the park custodian, Ramona was temporarily assigned to maintenance duties. During this time, the ruins preservation position was vacant and Ramona was paid from a maintenance account. The lapse salary was used to purchase new scaffolding equipment to replace worn and damaged equipment. During the time Ramona was not assigned to maintenance, she was actively engaged in the stabilization of the San Buenaventura Mission complex at Gran Quivira.

Ramona is a very experienced stabilization worker who provides direct on-site supervision for quality control and who routinely trains new hires. She is experienced in many aspects of ruins preservation work.

Training: Ramona participated in OSHA Fall Protection training.

Laser scanning at the Mission of San Gregorio at Abó, Salinas Pueblo Missions National Monument.
Photo: Courtesy Salinas Pueblo Missions National Monument

Marc A. LeFrançois, Exhibit Specialist
FY 2003 Position

Because Marc has been filling the vacancy left by Phil Wilson, who left in October, 2007, this position was vacant during part of FY 2008. His duties this year included facility management, so time spent performing maintenance duties was charged to a maintenance account.

Marc managed all resource activities within the park, including the documentation of the Abó Mission, and the implementation of preservation treatments at San Buenaventura at Gran Quivira. He also managed all park personnel involved with resource preservation.

Marc is skilled in architectural conservation and historic trade skills as well as in resource management.

Training: All of Marc's FY 2008 training involved annual management training requirements.

Vacant, Archeologist
FY 1999 Position

This position was originally filled as a preservation specialist but has been converted to an archeologist.

With the departure of Phil Wilson, this position was vacant for most of FY 2008. The lapse salary was used to purchase new scaffolding equipment to replace damaged and worn equipment. The park plans to refill this position in FY 2009.

Vacant, Archeologist
FY 2000 Position

This position was originally filled as a craft specialist but has been converted to an archeologist.

This position was vacant during part of FY 2008. The lapse salary was used to purchase new scaffolding equipment to replace damaged and worn equipment. The park plans to refill this position in FY 2009.

Vacant, Maintenance Worker (Ruins Preservation)
FY 2003 Position

This position was vacant for all of FY 2008. The lapse salary was used to purchase new scaffolding equipment to replace damaged and worn equipment. The park plans to refill this position in FY 2009.

VANISHING TREASURES PROJECT FUNDING

Project Name: Implement Preservation Treatments at the San Buenaventura Mis-

The Mission of Purísima Concepción at Quarai with a large kiva in the foreground, Salinas Pueblo Missions National Monument.
Photo: Randall Skeirik

sion Complex

PMIS Number: 37683

Project Summary: This project involved the stabilization of the San Buenaventura Mission at Gran Quivira, which ran from March to the end of the fiscal year.

Project Budget:

Total VT Project Funding:$125,000

Personnel:	$90,318
Vehicles:	$9,516
Travel/Training:	$970
Supplies/Materials:	$21,026
Equipment:	$0
Services/Contracts:	$2,918
Other:	$300

Project Accomplishments: This project implemented preservation strategies based on the intensive documentation and analysis of the San Buenaventura Mission complex that was performed in FY 2005. The treatments were based on an analysis of data obtained through 3-D laser scanning and mapping of the architectural remains and adjacent landscape. The scans were used to obtain accurate, basic metric data and to visualize the architecture in a 3-D digital environment. The geo-referenced laser scans were exported as shape files and attributed with various datasets including stabilization histories, environmental data, and condition assessment information. Spatial analysis then identified patterning in the rate and occurrence of deterioration and was used in establishing causal relationships.

Project work included the following:

- Soil and stone analyses of the existing mortar, wall stones, and adjacent terrain to develop different mortar mixes for intervention treatments. Mortars types included capping, repointing, and void filling, with variations as determined by chemical and moisture distribution occurrences;
- Geologic mapping of the area to identify depth to bedrock and subsurface anomalies;
- A vibration impact study, and;
- Review and analysis of the public use of the site and the park's interpretive program.

Using this data the park has completed several activities including the following:

- Identification of the primary sources of deterioration and the causal relationship between the manifestations of deterioration and its source(s);
- Development of appropriate preservation strategies to address the sources of deterioration and prioritized treatment strategies, and;
- Development of monitoring strategies to evaluate changes in site and environmental conditions and evaluate the effectiveness of treatment strategies.

Through this project, the park has implemented sustainable long-term preservation treatments based on a thorough understanding of the resource, its significance, its scientific and public value, and its place in the natural environment.

Vanishing Treasures
Texas

A failing retaining wall in the Corral of the Williams Ranch, Guadalupe Mountains National Park.   Photo: Randall Skeirik

◇ Big Bend National Park ◇ Fort Davis National Historic Site ◇
◇ Guadalupe Mountains National Park ◇ Lake Meredith National Recreation Area ◇
◇ San Antonio Missions National Historical Park ◇

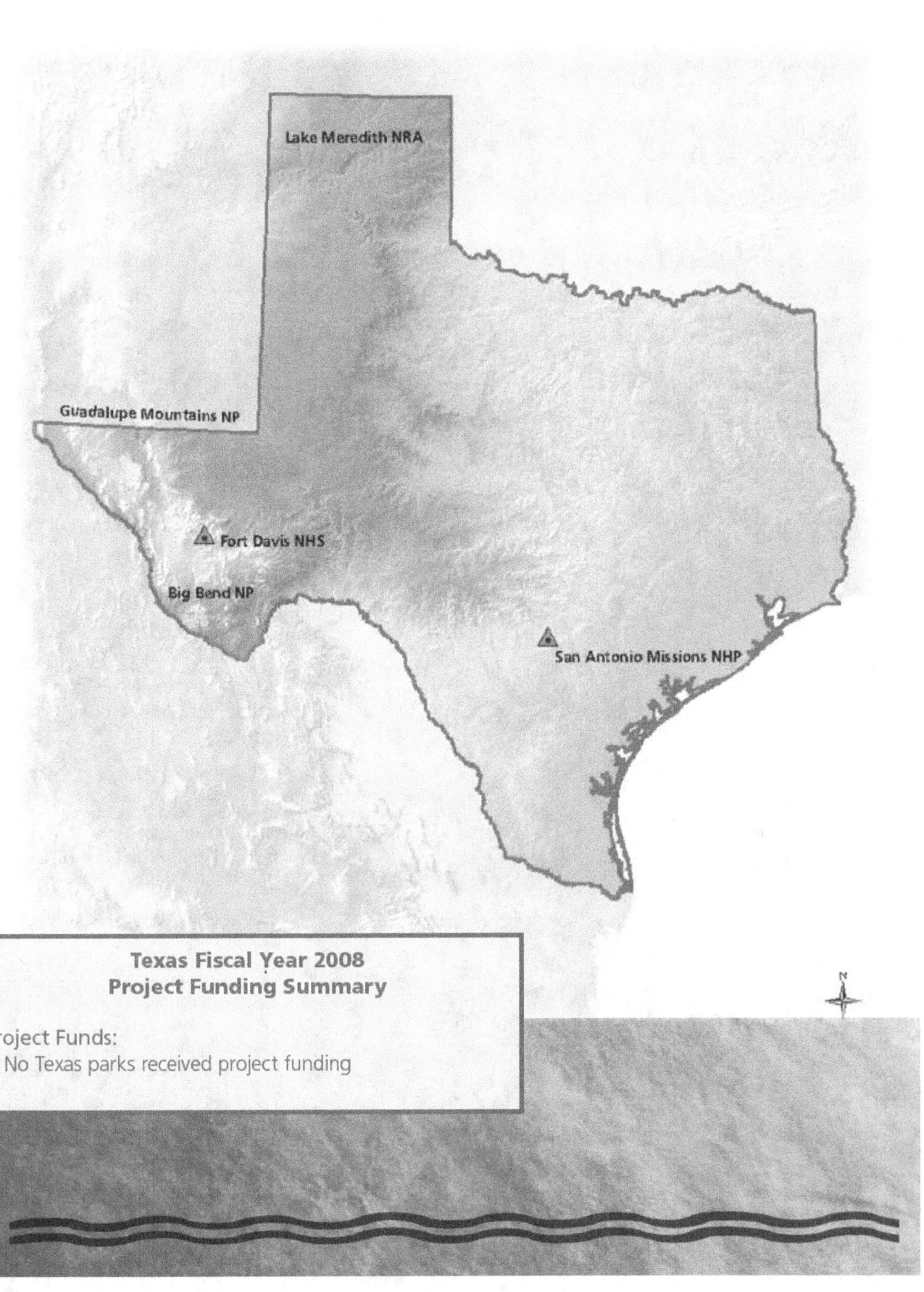

Lake Meredith NRA

Guadalupe Mountains NP

Fort Davis NHS

Big Bend NP

San Antonio Missions NHP

**Texas Fiscal Year 2008
Project Funding Summary**

Project Funds:
  No Texas parks received project funding

Fort Davis National Historic Site (FODA)

VANISHING TREASURES STAFF

Roy Catano, Masonry Worker
FY 2000 Position

Fort Davis National Historic Site did not report on Roy's activities for fiscal year 2008.

Miguel Estrada, Program Manager for Cultural Resource and Facility Division
FY 2000 Position

Fort Davis National Historic Site did not report on Mickey's activities for fiscal year 2008.

VANISHING TREASURES PROJECT FUNDING

Fort Davis National Historic Site did not receive project funding in FY 2008.

The porch of the post hospital, Fort Davis National Historic Site.
Photo: Randall Skeirik

Mission Concepción, San Antonio Missions National Historical Park .
Photo: Randall Skeirik

San Antonio Missions National Historical Park (SAAN)

VANISHING TREASURES STAFF

Susan Snow, Archeologist
FY 1999 Position

San Antonio Missions National Historical Park did not report on Susan's activities for fiscal year 2008.

Dean Ferguson, Masonry Worker
FY 2000 Position

San Antonio Missions National Historical Park did not report on Dean's activities for fiscal year 2008.

Steve Siggins, Masonry Worker
FY 2003 Position

San Antonio Missions National Historical Park did not report on Steve's activities for fiscal year 2008.

VANISHING TREASURES PROJECT FUNDING

San Antonio Missions National Historical Park did not receive project funding in FY 2008.

Vanishing Treasures
Utah

Documenting a structure below the Turk's Head, Canyonlands National Park.   *Photo: Canyonlands National Park*

◇ Arches National Park ◇ Capitol Reef National Park ◇ Canyonlands National Park ◇
◇ Glen Canyon National Recreation Area ◇ Golden Spike National Historic Site ◇
◇ Hovenweep National Monument ◇ Natural Bridges National Monument ◇ Zion National Park ◇

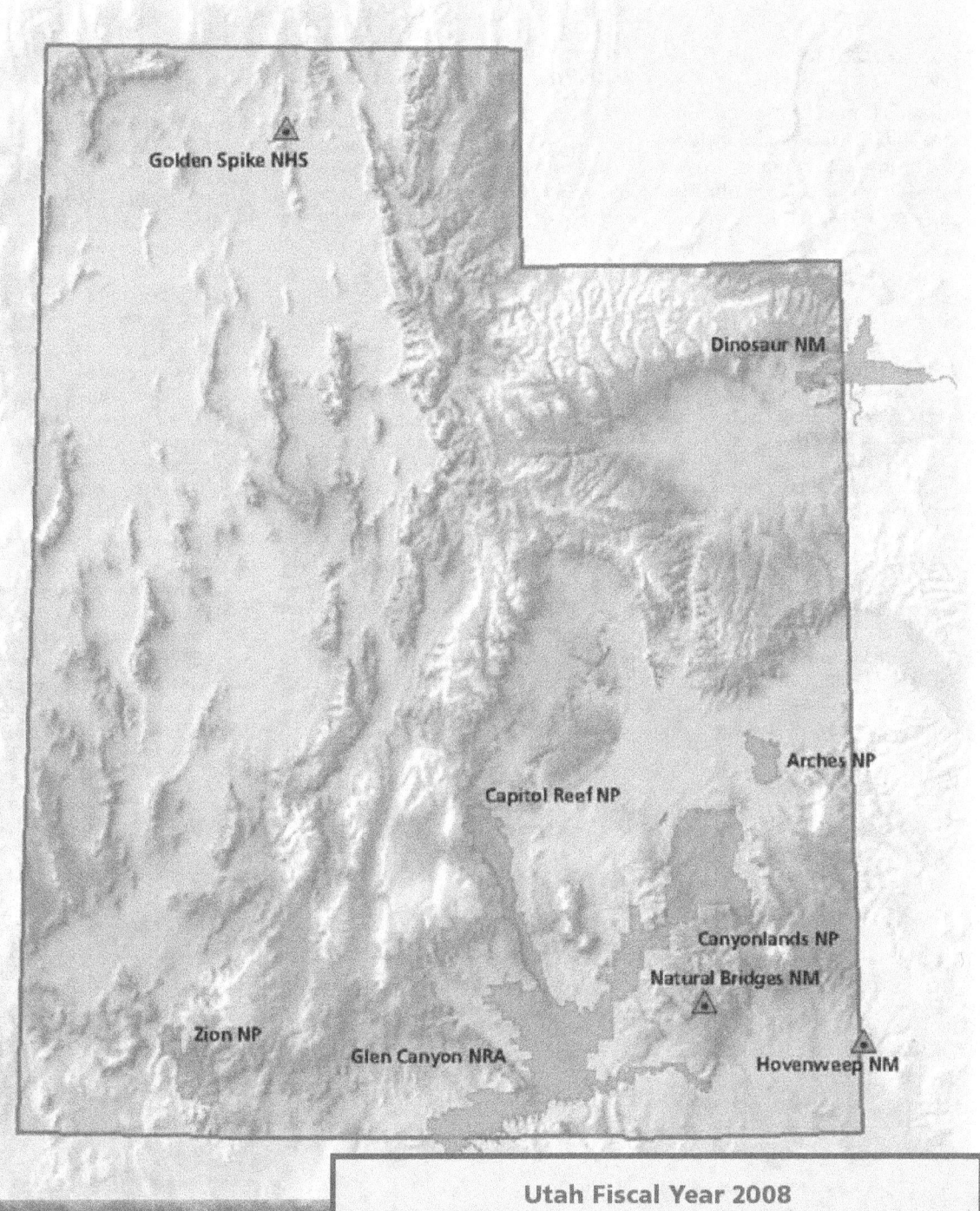

Golden Spike NHS

Dinosaur NM

Arches NP

Capitol Reef NP

Canyonlands NP

Natural Bridges NM

Zion NP

Glen Canyon NRA

Hovenweep NM

Utah Fiscal Year 2008
Project Funding Summary

Project Funds:
   Canyonlands National Park: $125,000
   Glen Canyon National Recreation Area: $58,600

Canyonlands National Park (CANY)

Canyonlands is part of the Southeast Utah Group (SEUG) that also includes Arches National Park, and Hovenweep and Natural Bridges National Monuments.

VT Challenges and Successes: The biggest challenge of the year was the procurement and transport of a 1,200-pound cottonwood log for the Fort Bottom Cabin. This effort involved personnel from the river shop/ law enforcement, search and rescue, maintenance, trails, resource management, the Southwest Conservation Corps, and park personnel from other districts of Canyonlands. The log was floated down the river, attached to a high-line system and transported up from the river to the cabin. The moving of the log was a good exercise in rigging for future search and rescue purposes.

Safety: The Vanishing Treasures crew from the Southeast Utah Group completed all work during this field season without incident. This included use of boats for transport on the rivers, hiking up and down steep talus slopes to access sites, carrying heavy stabilization materials and equipment, and

the set-up and breakdown of field camps. Additionally, a 1,200-pound replacement log for the Fort Bottom Cabin was moved to the site and successfully installed without any accidents or safety problems. Both phases of the project were planned and conducted at a time of the year when there were no high-water issues on the rivers, and summer heat was not a factor.

VANISHING TREASURES STAFF

Sue Eininger, Archeologist
FY 2002 Position

In 2008, Sue completed the report entitled "2004-2006 River Corridor Architecture and Rock Art Survey." Part of the field effort for this report was funded by the Vanishing Treasures Program. The 400-page manuscript summarizes the activities and results of a three-year site documentation and condition assessment project along the Green and Colorado Rivers in Canyonlands National Park. Sue had served on the field crew for the duration of the project and was the logical choice to author the document.

In addition to her writing duties, Sue also participated as a field crew member on the River Corridor Ruins Stabilization Project, a Vanishing Treasures-funded project to

address the recommendations made in the River Corridor Architecture and Rock Art Survey. Sue assisted other staff in the stabilization of a number of sites along the Green and Colorado Rivers.

Sue has extensive experience in archeological site documentation, condition assessment, structure stabilization, database management, and report writing.

Pat Flanigan, Exhibit Specialist
FY 2002 Position

In 2008, Pat performed condition assessment work on Vanishing Treasures resources in both Arches and Canyonlands National Parks. He completed rodent-proofing at the Wolfe Ranch Cabin and worked with maintenance staff and volunteers to successfully solve long-term drainage problems around the base of the Cabin.

Pat continued the task of updating List of Classified Structure (LCS) records, updating documentation and condition information for 11 previously recorded sites in the Salt Creek Archeological District of Canyonlands National Park, and entering associated information into both the Archeological Site Management Information System (ASMIS) and the LCS databases. Pat was

View down the Green River, Canyonlands National Park.
Photo: Courtesy Canyonlands National Park

also responsible for all photographic data processing related to the LCS work.

Pat has extensive experience in site documentation, condition assessment, and data entry.

VANISHING TREASURES PROJECT FUNDING

Project Name: Stabilize Threatened VT Sites in the River Corridors

Project Summary: The River Corridor Vanishing Treasures Stabilization and Documentation Project in Canyonlands National Park took place in two stages, from March through May and again in September, 2008. Six prehistoric sites were stabilized in the spring and an historic cabin located on the Green River was stabilized in September. Southeast Utah Group monitoring forms were updated to reflect the change in condition after the preservation work was completed. Additional work completed during this project included archeological site documentation, site monitoring, and site assessment for future stabilization or documentation needs.

Project Budget:
Total VT Project Funding: $125,000

Personnel:	$47,250
Vehicles:	$0
Travel/Training:	$8,229
Supplies/Materials:	$6,325
Equipment:	$4,430
Services/Contracts:	$0
Other:	$58,690

Project Accomplishments: Six prehistoric sites--four located on the Green River at Turk's Head and Jasper Canyon and two sites on the Colorado River at Dog Leg and Monument Canyons--were selected for stabilization treatments through this project. These sites, some of the most heavily visited by the recreational public, were exhibiting serious degradation from both human and natural impacts. Stabilization work included the repointing of eroded masonry joints, wedging of dry-laid masonry, backfilling, and limited graffiti removal.

The stabilization of the historic cabin at Fort Bottom on the Green River was treated as a separate phase of the project because of the different approaches used to preserve masonry and wooden structures. Based on a condition assessment prepared by Randy Skeirik, VT Historical Architect, work on the cabin included the removal of the roof-fall material from the interior, replacement of an eroded sill log, insertion of dowels into the corners of the structure, pinning the rafter tails to the beam of the porch/ramada, application of Boracare to the lowermost logs on the cabin, setting Impel rods into the top beams, repair of the entry door, and the installation of Dutchman-type splices into rotted areas on the tops of two purlins. Jake Barrow, VT Exhibit Specialist, was recruited to direct and assist with the historic preservation work. The sill log replacement turned out to be a collaborative effort that engaged personnel from numerous divisions throughout Canyonlands and other districts of the park.

In addition to conducting preservation maintenance on these seven sites, project funding also allowed the monitoring of two previously recorded sites and the archeological documentation of an additional 17 prehistoric sites, four of which received minimal stabilization during recording. Sites that were documented during this project were primarily those that were readily visible along the river corridors and had had minimal if any previous documentation. Finally, six archeological sites were visited and assessed for potential future stabilization and/or documentation needs.

All of the documented sites were entered into the SEUG archeological database and the park-wide ASMIS database. All but two of the documented sites are considered eligible for the National Register of Historic Places.

Stabilization work being conducted at the Fort Bottom Cabin, Canyonlands National Park.
Photo: Courtesy Canyonlands National Park

Glen Canyon National Recreation Area (GLCA)

VANISHING TREASURES ACCOMPLISHMENTS AND CHALLENGES

VT Challenges and Successes: The management of the VT Program at Glen Canyon suffered from the concurrent loss of both our Chief of Cultural Resources and our Vanishing Treasures Archeologist during FY 2007. Rosemary Sucec has recently filled the Chief of Cultural Resources position; and archeological technician Thann Baker is currently working under a Student Career Experience Program (SCEP) appointment.

Consultation: Glen Canyon maintains consultation with up to twelve tribes and two State Historic Preservation Offices (SHPOs). In FY 2008, a programmatic agreement was signed between the Utah SHPO and GLCA, outlining the procedures for expedited compliance and consultation.

Safety: Most of the cultural resources at GLCA are located in rugged and difficult-to-access backcountry areas. Helicopter transport and an extended field season were required to accomplish this year's VT project. Helicopter training, backcountry plan protocols, and general safety awareness ensured an accident-free year.

VANISHING TREASURES STAFF

Thann Baker, Archeological Technician FY 2002 Position

This position was vacant during part of FY 2007. Lapse salary was diverted to satisfy other urgent park needs.

In FY 2008, Thann accompanied and assisted the Mesa Verde National Park archeological conservation crew in conducting condition assessment and architectural documentation of six sites in Cow Canyon in the Escalante River Basin in Glen Canyon National Recreation Area.

As a full-time student, Thann spent a good part of the year finishing his Master's thesis: an architectural analysis of storage facilities in the Escalante River Basin, providing a cultural and temporally sensitive typology of construction techniques.

Thann is trained in VT documentation techniques and, through cooperative agreements, has led condition assessment and architectural documentation crews at both Glen Canyon and Walnut Canyon National Monument. He is proficient both in the

Brian Culpepper, Chris Kincaid, and Thann Baker discuss site conditions in Cow Canyon, Glen Canyon National Recreation Area.
Photo: Courtesy Glen Canyon National Recreation Area

field and in the laboratory and has experience with geographic information systems (GIS), mapping with AutoCAD, Total Station, and global positioning systems (GPS), as well as with image production and conducting geophysical surveys.

VANISHING TREASURES PROJECT FUNDING

Project Name: Cow Canyon Archeological Site Condition Assessment and Architectural Documentation

PMIS Number: 116048

Project Summary: This project involved condition assessment and cyclic maintenance treatment for selected structural sites in Cow Canyon, a remote left-bank tributary of the Escalante River. Selected sites included Mud Granary, Tunnel Granary, Perfect Ruin, Covered Pot Alcove, Seven Step Kiva, and Gourd Grotto.

Project Budget:
Total VT Project Funding: **$58,600.00**

Personnel:	$0
Vehicles:	$0
Travel/Training:	$0
Supplies/Materials:	$0
Equipment:	$0
Services/Contracts:	$58,584
Other:	$0

Project Accomplishments: Work was initiated in June, 2008 by the archeological conservation crew of Mesa Verde National Park

(MEVE), accompanied by GLCA Archeological Technician Thann Baker. During the first year, accomplishments included the assessment and architectural documentation of the six sites identified in the original Scope of Work as well as more brief stabilization assessments of two additional sites: Nino Presidio (42KA2796) and The Watchtower (42KA2690). Fieldwork was conducted with an eight-member crew from MEVE and one Glen Canyon NRA staff member over ten days.

As a result, stabilization treatments have been recommended for four of the original six sites (Seven Step Kiva, Mud Granary Ruin, Tunnel Granary, and Perfect Ruin) and one of the two additional sites that were assessed (Nino Presidio).

Year-one deliverables will include completed data entry; the production of AutoCAD maps and orthorectified digital imagery; updating of the archeological sites management information system (ASMIS) site records for all eight sites to meet NPS standards for completeness, accuracy, and reliability; and a completed cyclic Maintenance Plan for each structure. The Cyclic Maintenance Plan will describe the original fabric, current condition, threats, recommended maintenance cycle, potential for loss or catastrophic failures, and recommendations for monitoring and maintenance for each site.

Hovenweep National Monument (HOVE)

Hovenweep is part of the Southeast Utah Group (SEUG) that also includes Canyonlands and Arches National Parks, and Natural Bridges National Monument.

VANISHING TREASURES STAFF

Noreen R. Fritz, Archeologist
FY 2002 Position

Noreen serves as the preservation archeologist for all of the parks in the Southeast Utah Group.

She was the project director for a Vanishing Treasures stabilization and documentation project along the Green and Colorado Rivers in Canyonlands National Park in FY 2008. This project followed through with management recommendations made during the 2004-2006 River Corridor Architectural and Rock Art Survey project (also funded by Vanishing Treasures).

Additionally, Noreen updated documentation on several large Puebloan architectural complexes that are part of the Square Tower Group at Hovenweep National Monument. This completed the final set of Hovenweep records for the List of Classified Structures database. At the Cajon unit of Hovenweep, Noreen directed a group of Sierra Club volunteers conducting preservation maintenance (repointing) for a second year.

At Natural Bridges National Monument (NABR), Noreen led archeological site tours at Kachina Bridge Ruin and Horsecollar Ruins as part of the park's centennial celebration. She also conducted a training session for the NABR staff to implement a staff monitoring program for heavily visited archeological sites in the monument, and, in December 2007, she monitored fuel reduction activities along the entrance road to Natural Bridges.

Noreen's specialties include ruins preservation, condition assessment, List of Classified Structures (LCS), and archeological site documentation.

Training: Noreen attended the Intermountain Regional Conference for Comprehensive Resource Stewardship held in Tucson, Arizona in May, 2008. She also received on-the-job training from Jake Barrow in historic cabin stabilization techniques.

Laura Martin, Exhibit Specialist
FY 2002 Position

In FY 2008, Laura performed documentation, condition assessments, and stabilization of prehistoric Puebloan architectural sites along the Colorado and Green Rivers in Canyonlands National Park--a project that was funded through the Vanishing Treasures Program. Using AutoCAD and Adobe Photoshop software, Laura developed stabilization documentation of this project from photogrammetric images that she produced during the 2004-2006 phase of the project. These images will be used for architectural analysis, archival documentation, and for long-term monitoring activities.

At Hovenweep National Monument, as part of the update to the List of Classified Structures database, Laura updated site documentation of several large prehistoric Puebloan architectural sites at the Square Tower Unit. Much of this work focused on mapping and recording structures, features, and artifact scatters that had previously not been recorded or described within the site record. She also conducted a literature search of these sites to update legacy data within the Archeological Sites Management Information System (ASMIS) and updated archeological data and management recommendations.

At Natural Bridges National Monument, Laura and seasonal employee Erin Lewis mapped a series of architectural and rock art sites around the base of Ruin Rock and performed checks on previously recorded data.

In addition to her VT duties, Laura periodically conducted National Historic Preservation Act compliance work and monitored construction activities and fuel reduction projects at both Hovenweep and Natural Bridges. Laura also conducted public archeological tours of Horsecollar Ruin and Kachina Bridge Ruin as part of Natural Bridges National Monument's Centennial Celebration.

Laura is skilled in the application and operation of Total Station and global positioning system (GPS) mapping technology. She is also skilled in the production of integrated mapping products using geographical information systems (GIS), AutoCAD, Tripod Data Systems, and Adobe Photoshop software. She is highly experienced in performing site-wide archeological inventory documentation, architectural documentation, condition assessments, and stabilization mitigations.

Training: In the spring, Laura attended the Intermountain Region Conference for Comprehensive Resource Stewardship in Tucson, AZ. In March, 2008, Laura completed her wildland firefighter refresher.

VANISHING TREASURES PROJECT FUNDING

Hovenweep National Monument did not receive project funding this year.

A structure in the Holly Group, Hovenweep National Monument.
Photo: Randall Skeirik

Vanishing Treasures
Wyoming

Buildings along Officer's Row Fort Laramie National Historic Site.   *Photo: Courtesy Fort Laramie National Historic Site*

◇ **Fort Laramie National Historic Site** ◇

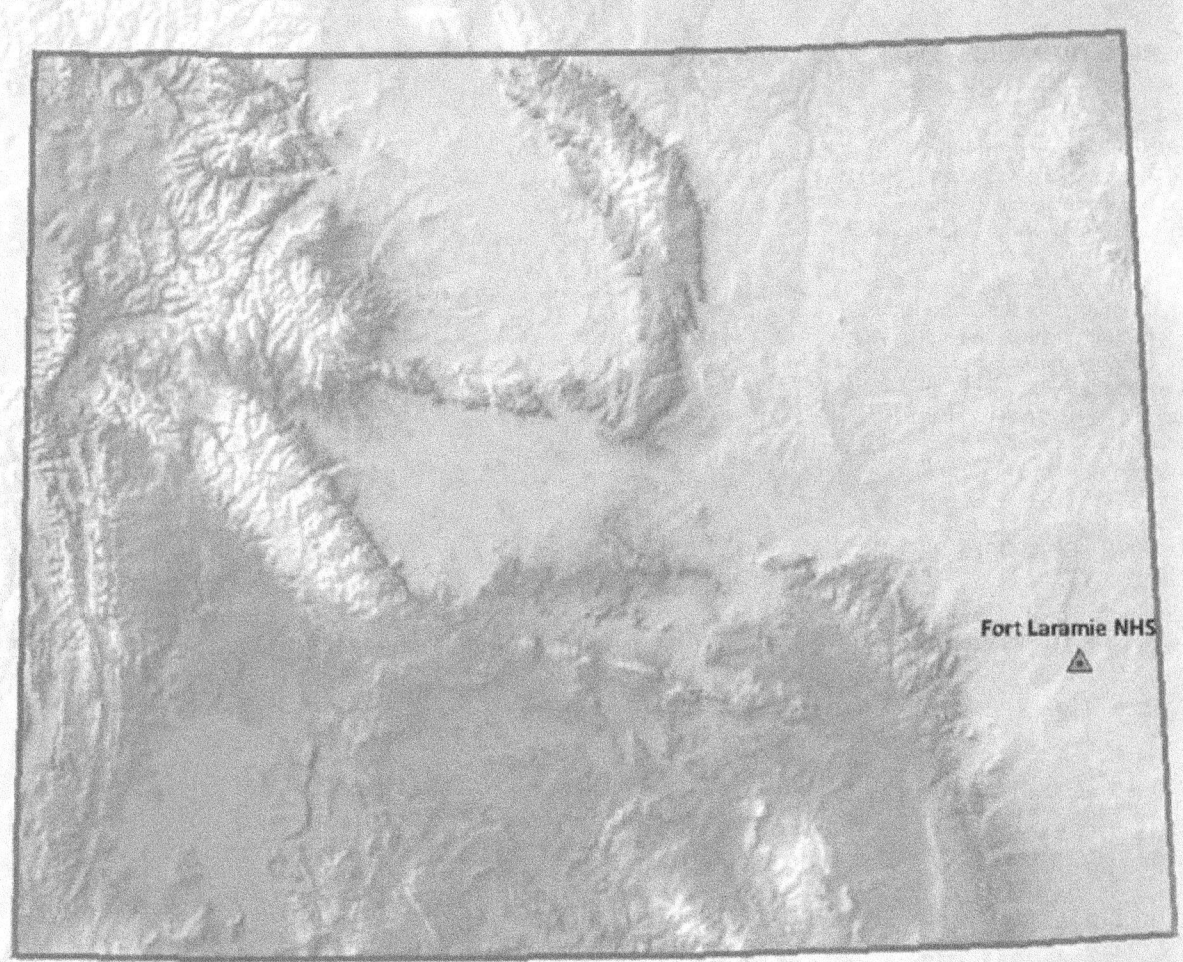

Fort Laramie NHS

**Wyoming Fiscal Year 2008
Project Funding Summary**

Project Funds:
No Wyoming park received project funding.

Fort Laramie National Historic Site (FOLA)

VANISHING TREASURES STAFF

Vacant
FY 2008 Position

Fort Laramie received a Vanishing Treasures-funded base increase this fiscal year for an Exhibit Specialist (Ruins Preservation). This new position has been developed and is in the course of being filled. This year's lapse salary was used to acquire a computer for the new position, an off-road utility vehicle for hauling VT employees and supplies to work sites, and various other VT-related supplies and materials. The remaining balance of funding was absorbed by other park maintenance needs after being offered to fellow VT parks.

VANISHING TREASURES PROJECT FUNDING

Fort Laramie National Historical Site did not receive project funding this year.

*A protective shelter coat being applied, Fort Laramie National Historic Site.
Photo: Courtesy Fort Laramie National Historic Site*

*A historic photo showing soldiers assembled on the parade grounds in 1883, Fort Laramie National Historic Site.
Photo: Fort Laramie National Historic Site*

Vanishing Treasures

Appendices

Appendix A:
Definition of Vanishing Treasures Resources .... *i*

Appendix B:
Terminology .... *i*

Appendix C:
Leadership Committee .... *ii*

Appendix D:
Advisory Group .... *ii*

Appendix E:
Annual and Cumulative Funding .... *iii*

Appendix F:
VT Fiscal Year 2008 Project Funding .... *iv*

Appendix A: Definition of Vanishing Treasures Resources

Vanishing Treasures Resources are defined as a structure or grouping of related structures that:
- Are in a "ruined" state.
- Have exposed intact fabric (earthen, stone, wood, etc.).
- Are not being used for their original function.
- Occupation and utilization have been interrupted or discontinued for an extended period of time.
- Are located in the arid West.
- Are the resources, or part of the resources, for which the park was created, are a National Historic Landmark, or listed on, or eligible for listing on, the National Register of Historic Places.

Examples of Vanishing Treasures Resources:
- Architectural remains that have intact historic fabric exposed at or above grade including: wall alignments, upright slabs, foundations, bins, cists, constructed hearths.
- Sub-grade architecture exposed through excavation or erosion (i.e., pithouses, dugouts, cists, etc.).
- Native American architectural structures (i.e., pueblos, cliff dwellings, hogans, wickiups, ramadas, corrals, earthen architecture, etc.).
- EuroAmerican architectural structures (i.e., churches, convents, forts, ranch-farm structures/homesteads, mine buildings, acequias or related features, kilns, etc.).

Examples of Non-Vanishing Treasures Resources:
- Sites with no exposed architecture or structural remains, (i.e., collapsed, buried, mounded, or otherwise not evident).
- Archeological or other sites with no architectural remains (i.e., lithic scatters, dumps, campsites, etc).
- Civilian Conservation Corps (CCC) and Civil Works Administration (CWA) buildings and features.
- Historic structures that are regularly maintained, and/or adaptively used, and fit within the Historic Structures/List of Classified Structures (LCS) definitions.
- Structures in use as National Park Service facilities (i.e., administrative buildings, trails, bridges, ditches, canals, etc).
- Mineshafts or caves, that do not have architectural/structural features.
- Pictographs, petroglyphs, rock art, etc., except if found in or on architectural structures.
- National Park Service or other reconstructed buildings or ruins (i.e., Aztec Great Kiva, Bents Old Fort).

> Note: Many of the traditionally associated communities to whom Vanishing Treasures resources/archeological sites hold importance, do not consider those sites to be unoccupied, out of use, or abandoned. "Ruins" are considered by some groups to be spiritually inhabited and are considered to be "in use" by virtue of being invoked in prayers, songs, stories, etc. They are considered dynamic parts of active cultural systems. While we use the term "ruins" and the associated definition, it is recognized that some communities do not use the term "ruin" nor consider the places to be unoccupied or out of use.

Appendix B: Terminology

Condition

Good - The site shows no clear evidence of major negative disturbance and deterioration by natural and/or human forces. The site's archeological values remain well-preserved, and no site treatment actions required in the near future to maintain its condition.

Fair - The site shows clear evidence of minor disturbance and deterioration by natural and/or human forces, and some degree of corrective action should be carried out fairly soon to protect the site.

Poor - The site shows clear evidence of major disturbance and rapid deterioration by natural and/or human forces, and immediate corrective action is required to protect and preserve the site.

Intensity of On-Site Erosion

Severe - The site will be significantly damaged or lost if action is not taken immediately.

Moderate - For an impact to be considered moderate, it must meet at least one of the following criteria:

The site will be significantly damaged or lost if action is not taken in the immediate future.

The site has been damaged and some integrity has been lost.

Low - The continuing effect of the impact is known but it will not result in significant or irreparable damage to the site.

None - The site has not been obviously impacted.

Integrity – Integrity refers to how much of the structure remains standing and intact. For example, a structure with only one intact, standing wall, would be given a value of 20% . A structure with all four walls standing and intact, plus an intact roof and floor, a 100% value would be given.

Stability – Stability refers to a wall or structures' state of equilibrium.

Stable - A structure that maintains consistency of composition and components with little or no sign of erosion that would lead to any form of structural degradation. The term stable can also be applied to structures that have essentially deteriorated to grade and thus have little or no standing structural remains above the ground surface that would be subject to further deterioration.

Partially Stable - A structure that exhibits signs of whole or partial degradation of the existing composition and components such that structural stability is threatened.

Unstable - A structure that has suffered damage from erosion such that structural collapse or complete degradation is imminent.

Appendix C: Leadership Committee

Vanishing Treasures Leadership Committee: 2006				
Representing	**Name**	**Term**	**Start Date**	**End Date**
Arizona	Brad Traver	3 Years	1/24/2006	May 2009
Arizona	Lee Baiza, Chair	3 Years	5/25/2005	May 2008
California/Nevada	Curt Sauer	3 Years	5/25/2005	May 2008
Colorado/Utah/Wyoming	Bruce Noble	2 Years	5/25/2005	May 2007
Colorado/Utah/Wyoming	Corky Hays	3 Years	5/25/2005	May 2008
New Mexico/Texas	Kayci Cook Collins	3 Years	1/24/2006	May 2009
New Mexico/Texas	Todd Brindle	2 Years	1/24/2006	August 2006
New Mexico/Texas	Darlene Koontz	2 Years	8/2006	
IMR	Sande McDermott	Permanent		
PWR	Stephanie Toothman	Permanent		
VT Program	Virginia Salazar-Halfmoon	Permanent		

Vanishing Treasures Leadership Committee: 2007				
Representing	**Name**	**Term**	**Start Date**	**End Date**
Arizona	Brad Traver	3 Years	2006	May 2009
Arizona	Lee Baiza, Chair	3 Years	2005	May 2008
California/Nevada	Curt Sauer	3 Years	2005	May 2008
Colorado/Utah/Wyoming	Corky Hays	3 Years	2005	May 2008
New Mexico/Texas	Kayci Cook Collins	3 Years	2006	May 2009
Colorado/Utah/Wyoming	Mitzi Frank	3 Years	2007	May 2010
IMR	Sande McDermott	Permanent		
PWR	Stephanie Toothman	Permanent		
VT Program	Virginia Salazar-Halfmoon	Permanent		

Vanishing Treasures Leadership Committee: 2008				
Representing	**Name**	**Term**	**Start Date**	**End Date**
Colorado/Utah/Wyoming	Corky Hays, Chair	3 Years	May 2008	May 2011
Arizona	Jason Lott	1 Year	May 2008	May 2009
Arizona	Lisa Carrico	3 Years	May 2008	May 2011
California/Nevada	Curt Sauer	3 Years	May 2008	May 2011
Colorado/Utah/Wyoming	Mitzi Frank	3 Years	May 2007	May 2010
New Mexico/Texas	Kayci Cook Collins	3 Years	May 2006	May 2009
New Mexico/Texas	Marie Frias	3 Years	May 2008	May 2011
IMR	Sande McDermott	Permanent		
PWR	Stephanie Toothman	Permanent		
VT Program	Virginia Salazar-Halfmoon	Permanent		
VT Program	Preston Fisher	Ex-officio		
VT Program	Randall Skeirik	Ex-officio		
VT Program	Jake Barrow	Ex-officio		

Appendix D: Advisory Group

As a result of the costs associated with maintaining the advisory group and the difficulty of arranging meetings, the VT Leadership Committee voted to dissolve the advisory group. Instead, ad hoc groups will be created to address specific needs or problems.

Appendix E: Annual and Cumulative Funding

Vanishing Treasures Annual and Cumulative Funding
FY 1998 through FY 2008

		VT Program Components			Total VT Program Expenditures	VT Park Base Increases		Total Base Increases	One-Year Personnel Funding³	Grand Total (Program plus Base)
		Projects	Training²	Management		Personnel	Additional¹			
FY 1998	Annual Budget	505,300	31,700	10,000	547,000	453,000	0	453,000	0	1,000,000
	Cumulative Total	505,300	31,700	10,000	547,000	453,000	0	453,000	0	1,000,000
FY 1999	Annual Budget	627,600	40,000	44,000	711,600	585,000	237,000	822,000	0	1,533,600
	Cumulative Total	1,132,900	71,700	54,000	1,258,600	1,038,000	237,000	1,275,000	0	2,533,600
FY 2000	Annual Budget	814,600	0	56,000	870,600	795,000	0	795,000	0	1,665,600
	Cumulative Total	1,947,500	71,700	110,000	2,129,200	1,833,000	237,000	2,070,000	0	4,199,200
FY 2001	Annual Budget	973,000	0	60,000	1,033,000	236,000	0	236,000	0	1,269,000
	Cumulative Total	2,920,500	71,700	170,000	3,162,200	2,069,000	237,000	2,306,000	0	5,468,200
FY 2002	Annual Budget	1,038,000	0	60,000	1,098,000	435,000	0	435,000	0	1,533,000
	Cumulative Total	3,958,500	71,700	230,000	4,260,200	2,504,000	237,000	2,741,000	0	7,001,200
FY 2003	Annual Budget	1,031,000	0	60,000	1,091,000	600,000	0	600,000	0	1,691,000
	Cumulative Total	4,989,500	71,700	290,000	5,351,200	3,104,000	237,000	3,341,000	0	8,692,200
FY 2004	Annual Budget	997,400	0	60,000	1,057,400	375,000	0	375,000	0	1,432,400
	Cumulative Total	5,986,900	71,700	350,000	6,408,600	3,479,000	237,000	3,716,000	0	10,124,600
FY 2005	Annual Budget	1,030,700	0	60,000	1,090,700	0	0	0	300,000	1,390,700
	Cumulative Total	7,017,600	71,700	410,000	7,499,300	3,479,000	237,000	3,716,000	300,000	11,515,300
FY 2006	Annual Budget	1,024,000	0	60,000	1,084,000	0	0	0	260,000	1,344,000
	Cumulative Total	8,041,600	71,700	470,000	8,583,300	3,479,000	237,000	3,716,000	560,000	12,856,300
FY 2007	Annual Budget	1,024,000	0	60,000	1,084,000	0	0	0	0	1,084,000
	Cumulative Total	9,065,000	71,700	530,000	9,667,300	3,479,000	237,000	3,716,000	560,000	13,940,300
FY 2008	Annual Budget	1,024,000	0	60,000	1,084,000	0	0	0	0	1,084,000
	Cumulative Total	10,089,000	71,700	590,000	10,751,300	3,479,000	237,000	3,716,000	560,000	15,024,300

Notes:
[1] $156,000 base increase for one park for personnel and an $81,000 park base increase.
[2] Between FY 1999 and FY 2004 training costs were added to the total cost for personnel and included in base increases. Beginning in FY2005 training funds will be deducted from project funds.
[3] In FY 2005 and FY 2006 personnel funding was for one year only and did not represent a permanent increase in park base funding. After FY 2006 the Program no longer provided money of any kind for personnel.

Appendix F: FY 2009   Project Funding

Appendix F: VT Fiscal Year 2009 Project Funding

				PMIS Allocation	
FY 2009 PROGRAM STATUS VANISHING TREASURES PROGRAM-FUND 01 TOTAL PROGRAM PROJECTED ALLOCATION				$1,078,000	
Less Region Assessment of 1.5% (1,078,000.00 x .01 = 10,780)				$10,780	
TOTAL AVAILABLE				$1,067,220	

Park	Account Number	PMIS Number	Project Name	PMIS Allocation	Adjustment Increase/Decrease
IMRO	7481-0504-CYA		VT Program Funds	$60,000	$ 0.00
WUPA	7470-0902-CYA	123846	Formal Condition Assessment of Fourth Fort Site Complex (WACA 10, 156, 211, 216, 217), Walnut Canyon	$118,467	$ 0.00
GRCA	8213-0901-CYA	121247	Vanishing Treasures Condition Assessments of Architectural Sites in the Desert View District	$84,124	$ 0.00
CAGR	8610-0901-CYA	123754	Compound A Preservation	$117,197	$ 0.00
MOCA	8650-0901-CYA	134753	Documentation and Stabilization of 14 Sites at Montezuma Well	$61,200	$ 0.00
CANY	1344-0901-CYA	92852	Conduct Condition Assessments at 15 VT Sites in Salt Creek to Comply with the Corrective Action Plan	$123,200	$ 0.00
ZION	1596-0901-CYA	35205	Historic Sites Protection Plan	$58,516	$ 0.00
BAND	7127-0901-CYA	121601	Vanishing Treasures: Documentation and Conservation of Tsankawi Cavates FY10	$125,000	$ 0.00
AZRU	7380-0801-CYA	116535	Replace Three Protective Roofs at West Ruin	$25,380	$ 0.00
AZRU	7380-0901-CYA	37548	Preserve Ancient Earthen Plaster at Aztec West Ruin	$44,650	$ 0.00
WUPA	7470-0901-CYA	123612	Repair Drainage System and Backfill Selected Areas of Wupatki Pueblo.	$120,380	$ 0.00
MOJA		120263A	Conduct Condition Assessment and Prepare Treatment Plan for Bighorn Mine Residence	$4,086	Requested $34,963
DEVA	8136-0901-CYA	116962A	Repair Keane Wonder Mine Tramway	$125,000	$0.00
			TOTAL ALLOCATED	$1,067,200.00	
			AMOUNT UNALLOCATED	0	
			TOTAL PROJECT FUNDING FOR FY 2009 ($1,067,000 less $60,000 Program Funds)	$1,007,200.00	

Arizona

1 Canyon de Chelly National Monument
2 Casa Grande Ruins National Monument
3 Coronado National Memorial
4 Fort Bowie National Historic Site
5 Grand Canyon National Park
6 Montezuma Castle National Monument
7 Navajo National Monument
8 Organ Pipe Cactus National Monument
9 Petrified Forest National Park
10 Saguaro National Park
11 Tonto National Monument
12 Tumacacori National Historical Park
13 Tuzigoot National Monument
14 Walnut Canyon National Monument
15 Wupatki National Monument

California / Nevada

16 Death Valley National Park
17 Joshua Tree National Park
18 Mojave National Preserve
19 Manzanar National Historic Site

Colorado

20 Colorado National Monument
21 Dinosaur National Monument (Also Utah)
22 Mesa Verde National Park

New Mexico

23 Aztec Ruins National Monument
24 Bandelier National Monument
25 Chaco Culture National Historical Park
26 El Malpais National Monument
27 El Morro National Monument
28 Fort Union National Monument
29 Gila Cliff Dwellings National Monument
30 Pecos National Historical Park
31 Salinas Pueblo Missions National Monument

Texas

32 Big Bend National Park
33 Fort Davis National Historic Site
34 Guadalupe Mountains National Park
35 Lake Meredith National Recreation Area
36 San Antonio Missions National Historical Park

Utah

37 Arches National Park
38 Capitol Reef National Park
39 Canyonlands National Park
40 Glen Canyon National Recreation Area
    (Also Arizona)
41 Golden Spike National Historic Site
42 Hovenweep National Monument
    (Also Colorado)
43 Natural Bridges National Monument
44 Zion National Park

Wyoming

45 Fort Laramie National Historic Site

If you have questions about the Vanishing Treasures
Program, please contact Program Manager
Virginia Salazar-Halfmoon (Virginia_Salazar-Halfmoon@NPS.gov)

Vanishing Treasures Parks

National Park Service
U.S. Department of the Interior

Vanishing Treasures, 2009

EXPERIENCE YOUR AMERICA™

www.ingramcontent.com/pod-product-compliance
Lightning Source LLC
Chambersburg PA
CBHW080516290526
45790CB00006B/2196